# KERRY KATONA

## *Whole Again*

### LOVE, LIFE AND ME

# KERRY KATONA

## Whole Again

### LOVE, LIFE AND ME

MIRROR BOOKS

*I want to dedicate this book to Molly, Lilly, Heidi, Max and my little girl DJ. To my first born, Molly, for being one of my biggest rocks, she's got my sense of humour and whenever we're together we have the best laughs. Me and my Lilly are so alike it's scary, she's so stubborn but also so wise. My Heidi is the most beautiful little girl in the world, and for all of her insecurities I want her to know how much strength she's given me. My Max, the only true man I'll ever love with the most wicked sense of humour, not everyone gets it but I do. And lastly my DJ, she's my pride and joy and she'll always be my baby. I want you all to know that you're the reason I open my eyes every day.*

*And, of course, to my Ryan, need I say more.*

*But I also want to dedicate it to all of you lot who are buying this book. You've all supported me through my highs and lows. No matter if you're in the papers or not, everyone has their own shit to deal with, so I hope this book helps you all and gives you some hope if you need it.*

*Kerry*

MIRROR BOOKS

First published in Great Britain and Ireland in 2022 by
Mirror Books, a Reach PLC business,
5 St. Paul's Square, Liverpool, L3 9SJ.

www.mirrorbooks.co.uk
@TheMirrorBooks

Hardback ISBN: 9781915306043
eBook ISBN: 9781915306050

Photographic acknowledgements:
Alamy, Kerry Katona personal collection

Written with Sarah Morton.
Design and production: Michael McGuinness
Editor: Chris Brereton

Printed and bound by CPI Group (UK) Ltd,
Croydon, CR0 4YY.

# Contents

# Acknowledgements

To Sarah Morton, who helped put my story into words. Thank you so much for all your hard work in helping me write this book, and thanks for always being on the other end of the phone throughout it all. It's been years – and it's been emotional.

Big shout out to my agents, Craig Johnson-Pass and Molly Pass from Unleashed Talent Management, who have been completely amazing. Your hard work and belief in me has proven I *can* get it right when it comes to managers. Thank you for everything you do.

My mum, Sue – I love you. Thanks for shaping me. Without the childhood I had, I wouldn't be the person I am today.

Dawn – you've been a bloody lifesaver for me and my family! You've been there for me through thick and thin, you've seen it all. And to our Lesley, I love you girls.

Danielle. Wow, I wish I'd had you in my life from day dot. But better late than never! In the 12 years I've known you, I've not had a better friend. You've never left my side. I love you and I love our girlie holidays. You're NEVER an embarrassment! You're bloody perfect.

To my extended family, you know who you are and I'm so thankful you're back in my life.

My gorgeous Ryan – the ying to my yang, the man who's completely balanced me out, helped me believe in myself again – thank you. Thank you for everything you do for our family. I love you so much.

And finally, this book would never have been written if it wasn't for my five beautiful kids. Molly, Lilly, Heidi, Max and DJ, you're my world. You are my everything. I would not be here today without you and that's a fact. All the grafting, it's all for you. You saved me. And I love you more than you'll ever know.

# *Prologue*

I close my eyes and clutch my baby daughter to my chest. Crouched inside a pitch black wardrobe, tears stream down my face while I try my hardest not to hyperventilate as I feel him getting nearer.

I just need to hide in here long enough so that he calms down. If I'm out of sight it'll give him time to chill out a bit and then maybe I won't get a hiding. If I can just last a little bit longer...

Oh please baby girl, don't cry. If Daddy hears you he'll know where we are – he'll find us and he'll drag me out of the wardrobe by my hair. He'll put his fists to my face again and you'll soon see the bruises, the same, familiar bruises I try so hard to hide, but ones I know your brother and sisters see. The ones that make them look at me with such sadness. If we utter one sound Mummy will get hurt again and everyone will be sad once more – and so we have to be as quiet as we can. Shh, baby girl. Please, shhhh…

It's an impossible situation. My husband, George, is on one again while we're on holiday in Cape Verde. He's lost his temper and as usual he's taking it out on me. As I cradle our daughter, Dylan-Jorge, I pray to a god I sometimes wonder exists. How is this my life? How the hell have I got myself back here?

Well, the answer is simple. This is exactly the life I expected for myself. Once upon a time I was a singer in a hugely popular girl band, married to the golden boy of pop, hanging out with the likes of Mariah Carey and Bryan Adams. But I was never comfortable in that world. Why? Because it wasn't me. All I knew before I was thrust into the showbiz bubble was pain. Abandonment. Abuse. Drugs. Alcohol. A mother who desperately needed mothering herself. And of course, as the public know, following my 'perfect' marriage to Westlife star Brian McFadden, one that ended with him cheating on me and ripping my heart out, I fell back into that murky world of drink, drugs and abandonment, enabled by a bad man whose only redeeming quality was the fact he fathered two of my beautiful, beloved children.

So of course I can't be surprised to find myself here, in my mid-thirties, now a mother of five, cowering in the wardrobe of a rented villa on the holiday I'm sharing with another abusive man, a man I love so much, a troubled ex-con, who ticks every box on my twisted list of romantic credentials.

I only have myself to blame. I made the choices that brought me to this point. I knew what I was doing when I started dating George Kay, a fella with a huge scar stretched across his stomach, a literal axe wound, the result of being stabbed in a fight, a grotesque marking he wore as a badge of honour. And, I hate to say it – something that actually turned me on. I loved the idea of a bad boy. Not like Mark Croft, my ex-husband, who is rotten to the core. I mean a sexy, dangerous, charismatic nutter who you know would protect you. Whose violent outbursts you could pass off as 'passionate'. Who wanted you so badly, no one else could have you. Or even speak to you. It's something I can't explain. But from the moment I reconnected with George, a boy I'd known from when we were teens hanging around Warrington, I knew I had to have him. And so here I am, barely three years later, hidden in a wardrobe, in a hell of my own making.

As my breathing quickens and I feel my little baby girl tense up in my arms, I begin to accept the inevitable. As he always does, George will find me. And he'll hurt me. And then following the beating he'll apologise and we'll make up and suddenly he'll sweep me up in his arms, begging for forgiveness and it'll all be worth it. 'Look how much he cares!' I'll say to myself, as I wince in pain from the cuts to my face. 'He's so passionate about me, he can't control himself! He loves me!'

The thought gives me a bizarre sense of comfort, and I realise the pattern will simply continue. So I give in. Firstly, I need to make sure my baby girl is safe – and while I know how much he loves her – I need to make sure she's out of harm's way. If I can just get her to safety, get her out of the way, I'll then accept the punishment coming to me. The sooner it's done, the sooner it's over. The sooner he'll be cradling me in those huge arms of his again, the sooner I'll forgive him, the sooner we'll be back to laughing and joking and staying up all night talking till my heart bursts with love once more.

So I open the wardrobe door, my little girl in my arms, and step into the light.

*****

Fast forward seven years and I sit down to write this book as a widow. George is gone, forever, taken at the age of just 39 in bizarre circumstances which even now, knowing him as I did, I still can't get my head around.

I'm in a happy, solid relationship with a man who I know in my heart I'll never leave. I have stability, money, a huge house full of laughter and bickering and dogs that jump up on my expensive yellow sofas with muddy paws. I have a career I've worked my arse off for. I'm back on the TV, running a hugely successful company with a fashion line, a dating app, a fitness business, I'm the creative director of a celebrity video brand called Thrillz and I unapologetically make a mint showing off my body on subscription website OnlyFans.

People in my past who tried to destroy me are now just a distant memory. Powerful men who I believe controlled my life and career have been given the middle finger as I've quietly taken back that control. And you know what? If they have a problem with it, they can come to the gates of my mansion and tell it to the intercom.

But it's been a long road to get here. And it's a road I'm still travelling. I'm not sure I'll ever fully recover from what I've been through, because the physical and mental scars left by George are just that, scars. They won't leave me. But perhaps that's a good thing. After all, you can't have regrets. Even the lowest points of my life – his death, hiding in that wardrobe with my littlest baby, watching as my first husband walked out on me – they all made me who I am today.

Yes of course it's a bloody cliché, but it's my truth. I go to bed at night grateful for every single tear I've shed over my lifetime. I've watched helplessly, from the age of just three years old as my mum tried to take her own life, I've stood shell shocked when receiving the gut wrenching phone call to tell me George – a man I'd left for good just a year earlier – had died on the floor of a Travel Inn with a stomach full of drugs. And every one of those moments has shaped me.

If I hadn't been subjected to such abuse, would I know the true value of the stability I have with my kind, gentle fiancé Ryan? If I hadn't made the mistakes I did, how would I know to advise my own children on making sure they don't follow suit?

Everything happens for a reason, to set you on a path to greater things. And I know I've made it. I was once a joke in the media. A punching bag whose 'car crash life' made headlines across the country. I was known as 'Cocaine Kerry' and I still believe to this day that gleeful newspapers had pre-prepared headlines ready to print in the event of my death. There was no thought for people's mental health back then or the idea that someone might truly be struggling, despite the fact I was always honest about my battle with bipolar syndrome. The attitude was very much: If you're in the public eye you're fair game.

Well I'm not fair game. I never was. I'm a mother, a businesswoman, a savvy grafter who's had to fend for herself all her life and who's raised five incredible kids, who all went to private school because I made sure I worked my arse off to get them there, with minimal help from their fathers.

Yes, I've made bad decisions but I own every single one of them. And now as I sit here, divorced twice, widowed once – just call me the modern day, female Henry VIII! – I'm slowly but surely starting to find peace within myself.

You know my background – my childhood and first two marriages have been well documented. But this is the first time I've laid bare the last decade of my life in such unflinching detail.

It was a significant period of time that brought me another

marriage, another baby, a secret pregnancy, debilitating health problems and a career slump I thought I'd never recover from. It was also responsible for several devastating deaths, which I know will stay with me for the rest of my life.

But it was also a time of hope. And as I sit and write this book, it continues to be. This is a story of strength. Of motherhood and unconditional love and rising up through the ashes of a fire which threatened to burn my very soul to cinders. It's a story of resilience and understanding, of overcoming struggles so many women like me are sadly all too familiar with. Struggles some are never fortunate enough to escape from.

It's a story of realisation and peace. And now, after years of desperately trying to find my way, I'm finally starting to feel – in the words of my most famous song – Whole Again.

This is how I got there.

# 1
# Good Times

The last book I wrote was published in late 2012. It ended on a hopeful note – I'd just got together with George Kay, the man who was to become my third husband and eventual father of my beautiful youngest child, Dylan-Jorge.

I was so happy back then. I can remember the feeling of pure joy as I looked forward to a future full of happiness. I was in love, I had four gorgeous kids and I'd exorcised the ghosts of the bad men who had plagued my life for so long. I was finally getting my happily ever after.

Or so I thought.

Back then I'd put two bad marriages behind me, one to Westlife singer Brian McFadden, which ended in 2006 when he cheated on me and left me to bring up our two daughters, Molly and Lilly-Sue, alone, and one to Mark Croft, who was my mum's drug dealer, believe it or not, and a taxi driver who was later convicted of running a cannabis farm.

At least with Mark he gave me two of my most precious gifts before we divorced in 2011, my daughter Heidi and son Max.

So for all the pain he caused me over the years – squandering my money, encouraging a godawful drug habit, leaving his kids high and dry and being a general twat – he did bless me with those two angels and for that I can't have too many regrets.

And then, after the Mark debacle, I met George.

Well, I say 'met' – we actually already knew each other from around Warrington, our home town.

I guess I should say 'then I fell in love with George'. And boy, did I fall hard.

I ended my second book floating on air. Sadly in the decade that's passed, I've fallen back down to earth with quite the bump. Life didn't exactly pan out as I'd hoped, at least not for a long time. It wasn't until I met my fiancé, Ryan Mahoney, dumped my manager and started standing on my own two feet again that I realised what true happiness and success looked like. What true *love* looked like. But I'll get to all of that.

Let me start at the beginning. Not my beginning – it's been well documented how I grew up with a mother who suffered from severe mental health issues, among other things, and how I was in and out of foster care and stripping for a living before finding fame as a singer in girl group Atomic Kitten.

I'm talking about the beginning of a period of time in my life which has defined me more so than any other. My journey back into the depths of Hell.

I'd known George since he was 14, when he was going out with a friend of mine. We both used to play rugby, if you can imagine me in a scrum!

His nickname was Gorgeous George, and he really was. He was so fit. 6ft 4 tall, massive arms, even when he was young he was a real intimidating guy to look at but if you ever spoke to him you'd see he was dead shy. And I guess he must have had a little thing for me, even when we were kids. He'd always flirt and giggle when we spoke, but I barely paid attention. I knew he was lovely looking, but I always just took the flirtation for banter. Case in point: When we were seventeen we were out one night with separate people and he approached me in whatever bar I'd managed to get into with my fake ID. He tapped me on the shoulder.

"Kerry..."

I spun around and looked up at those gorgeous dark eyes. "Yes?"

"Will you marry me?"

"Oh, piss off, you dickhead!"

It probably wasn't quite the reaction he was expecting but it caused him to crease up giggling and needless to say he got his way in the end!

He always made me laugh and over the years I'd occasionally see him out and about in town and say hello. And then of course I fell madly in love with Brian, became a huge pop star and spent my time hanging out with the likes of Mariah Carey instead. Soon enough the pretty boys of Warrington were a distant memory, including George.

But life has a funny way of working things out and I guess the universe had other plans for me because a few short years later fate dealt me a, let's say, *interesting* card.

It was September 2012 and I was celebrating my 32nd birthday with my mum, Sue, who had joined me and a couple of mates for cinema and drinks. I can't for the life of me remember what we saw, but the number one film at the box office that weekend was a movie called About Time, the super emotional love story in which the main character has – and I quote this from Wikipedia – 'the ability to time travel and tries to change his past in hopes of improving his future'.

Make of that what you will.

Anyway, after the pictures we headed to a bar, drinks were flowing and I soon made my way outside for a ciggy (I've since ditched the habit, in case you were wondering). Next thing I know, a very grown up, very gorgeous George came walking up to me.

"How ya doing George?" I asked, delighted to see that stunning face of his after so long. "What you been up to?"

There was a twinkle in his eye. "I've just come back from my holidays," he said.

"Ooh, look at you! Anywhere nice?" I was flirting outrageously, dragging on my cigarette like bloody Audrey Hepburn in Breakfast At Tiffany's.

"Six years in the clink," he replied. "Better than Spain." He was laughing.

Now don't get me wrong, I'm well aware that at this point any other woman would've turned on her heel and walked away.

But I was immediately hooked.

Knowing he'd been in prison – and now on probation – didn't worry me at all. Why would it? I'd spent my entire life around drug addicts and dealers, criminals and crooks. That was my normal. Hearing George joke about prison got me interested. In fact, it turned me on.

He said at the time it was for fraud. I later found out it was for kidnapping and torture as well. Turns out he chopped someone's toes off. But, as I say, I didn't realise that at the time, and to be honest I'm not sure it would've swayed me if I had!

# Good Times

Like I said, these sorts of people were the norm to me. It wasn't unheard of to know someone who'd been in prison, or been on drugs or who'd hit a woman. I come from a background where I've witnessed my own mum getting stabbed. I've shared drugs with her. Someone like George wasn't terrifying or scary, he was *normal*.

In fact, to me, this big brute of a man, who'd played professional rugby and had been a bouncer and bodyguard, represented safety and protection. I immediately felt relaxed in his company and I wanted him to look after me. Just looking at his stature and being in his presence, it was clear no one else would come near me when I was with him and I buzzed off that.

Plus, much like he did as a boy, he still made me laugh till my sides hurt.

We ended up snogging all night. After all this time of knowing him, even after that joke proposal years before, suddenly I saw him differently. I was falling hard and quickly.

So quickly in fact that the next day we went on a date go-karting, which led on to a third date at a hotel in Chester.

I was completely smitten. So smitten in fact that I was sad soon after when I found myself at the Jason Vale Juice Retreat in Turkey, a weight loss camp and a trip which had been planned for months. I didn't want to leave George, I was having way too much fun, and who needed a juice retreat anyway when the plentiful, energetic love-making was doing a fine job of keeping me in such great shape?!

But I'm never one to shirk, and this was a work commitment too, something I take very seriously. No matter what's going on in my life, if I've booked a job, I'll do it. Come hell or high water (or great sex!) I'll be there.

It didn't make too much difference, as George called me every single day when I was out there.

Having met my mum on my birthday and having sparked with her too, he actually visited her most days as well. To keep her company I guess. Maybe that was a sign of the possessiveness that was to come, the fact he would go and sit with her, waiting for me, rather than get on with his own life while I was gone.

But none of that crossed my mind back then. Instead I rushed back, feeling lighter and healthier than I had in years, and so excited to see him again.

I had no qualms about him meeting the children. No matter what people say about me, I've been very careful with introducing the kids to men. I've not had a lot of lovers and other than my husbands there's not been a lot of 'love' to speak of!

But with George something was so instant, I just knew I was in it for the long haul. He came to my home down south in Guildford – and never left.

For me it was love. I was absolutely on top of the world. The kids took to him straight away. Even now, Heidi and Max refer to him as 'Dad', that was the sort of bond they had immediately.

He was playful with them and acted like a big kid. He was such a charmer, my whole family was under his spell. Everything about him, the way he dressed, his smell, it was all perfect.

And, as I mentioned, he had that cracking sense of humour.

He'd come down from the bedroom with a pair of Spanx on his head just to make me giggle. I'd return the favour by sticking his boxers over my face and watch as he fell about, crying with laughter. It was daft, but so funny. We would make each other howl til we were both clutching our sides.

# Good Times

Of course, the laughs became forced over time. By the end of the relationship I was laughing just to please him. But back in the honeymoon period, I would be in stitches constantly.

And not the bad kind. Those were to come.

I remember the first time he told me he loved me. We'd just come back from Dubai, where we had the best time. I still look back on pictures of us from that holiday, one in particular where he's walking in a pair of white speedos on the beach, and I'm reminded how good we had it, when things were perfect.

Anyway, upon our return we were in bed at home. And he turned to me and simply said "I love you." I jokingly punched his arm and said, "Cheers luv, you're not so bad yourself!"

He creased up laughing and I couldn't stop beaming. My stomach had flipped, everything about him seemed so wonderful.

But let's not get it wrong – George was a troubled guy. And I knew that. He hadn't yet shown his violent side to me, but I knew there were demons there. Perhaps I thought I'd be the girl to banish them forever, but don't we all think that? Of course the reality is you can stave off the demon for so long, but it's always there. And at some point it will rear its ugly head.

George, a proud Black man, was adopted by a white couple and I think the uncertainty over his background – not knowing his true family or having any real link to his culture and identity – was something that messed him up, much like it does a lot of children. I'll never truly know for sure as it wasn't something we discussed much, but that feeling of not belonging was something we had in common from the off. I was in foster care from the age of 13 and I never knew my true father. George was adopted, same rules apply. We were kindred spirits.

The one thing I *didn't* realise early on was George was a drug addict. That was something he kept from me from the start. I knew he did steroids and I thought he dabbled with recreational drugs occasionally, but given my childhood that wasn't something that was particularly out of the norm and it certainly didn't warrant any worry from me.

But by the time we got engaged a few months later, when his mother took me aside and begged me not to marry him, I was well aware of his issues.

"He's a drug addict, Kerry. He'll destroy you. Don't do it," she had pleaded.

I remember at the time feeling sick to my stomach. Deep down, by that point, I instinctively knew she was right, but I was in love and I brushed it aside.

Still, when your own mum calls you out like that, you know you've got issues.

But I never would've called him an addict at the start. He wasn't even a massive drinker! It was obvious he'd put on a facade to woo me, to get me to fall in love with him, and it worked.

It was only later I realised just how much rubbish he was putting in his body, and the horrible effect it would have on his mind.

# 2

# The Violence Begins

It didn't take long for George's dark side to come out.

It was a few weeks after our first date, just after he declared his love for me in fact, and we very nearly broke up because of it.

Now, I've seen violence before. My mum was with a very abusive man for a long time, so witnessing women get beaten wasn't unusual. Of course it was scary, that feeling of being frightened for your life, terrified for the victim too – it never goes – but it was, as I've said, normal to me.

Nevertheless I was shaken to my core when George first showed his true colours.

Danielle Brown, my best friend in the world, was there, along with another amazing friend called Sharon Smith, who runs the GI Jane bootcamp. We were at home and it was the first time I'd introduced them to George. I was so excited for him and Danielle in particular to meet these two soulmates of mine, and it was important to me that Danielle liked him. I value her opinion, I always have. But even in the dark days that followed, when she would beg me to walk away from him as the two of us sat sobbing, I couldn't do it. That was the hold he had. But I digress…

Back to that night and Danielle and I were joking about this lad who'd asked me out on a date back when I was single and who'd planted a kiss on me that felt like a bloody washing machine. We were cracking up, like girls do, remembering this poor guy and I really thought George would see the funny side. After all, this all happened long before he was on the scene, it wasn't new information to George.

But instead of a smile, I saw his face change.

It was almost like a darkness had descended upon him. It was the most chilling thing. It was as if the light just went from his eyes.

"I'm going to bed," he said.

Oh shit.

"You alright love?" I asked, my throat suddenly dry.

He didn't answer and instead left the room and went upstairs.

I could see Danielle look at me as if to say, 'Oops! Someone's a bit jealous!' but she wasn't to know just how angry he was.

My heart sank. I didn't want to upset him! Why did I have to bang on about that lad kissing me?! The last thing I'd want is for George to feel sad!

I followed him to see if he was ok. And once we were both in the bedroom, he turned and threw his mobile phone right at the centre of my head at full force.

I was stunned. The pain didn't even register at first because I was so shocked at what had just happened. I couldn't believe he'd done that. And, seeing as this was the first time I'd experienced anything like that by his hand, I had the balls to stick up for myself.

# The Violence Begins

"What the bloody hell did you do that for!?" I yelled.

We started shouting at each other. And, to my enormous guilt even now, Molly told me she'd listened to it all and was very upset by what she'd heard. She was barely a teenager at this point and she'd never experienced anything like that before. Yes, Mark Croft and I had our moments, but my children had never witnessed any kind of violence or shouting. Now, the raised voices, the sheer terror of this huge man screaming at her mum, well Molly had never seen the like.

Immediately I knew what I had to do.

"Get out of my house and don't ever come back," I screamed. George duly obliged to the first part of that order.

Danielle came running to my side. I think she was as shocked as I was. We both sat there totally stunned, my head throbbing, my heart broken

Neither of us knew what to say in that moment, but I remember feeling all sorts of confusion, panic, sadness and doubt. Please, please don't let George be like the men my mother was with. Please.

Some time went by and I received a phone call from my mum, Sue. Turns out George had gone straight from mine over to hers.

I wasn't sure if I was relieved or angry or just completely confused by the fact he had the balls to do that to me and then go seek solace with MY mother!

"Kerry, he really loves you and he's dead sorry," she said, matter of factly as she puffed on a ciggy. I suppose she'd seen all this before. It was no doubt a minor incident to her, not even worthy of any drama.

"I don't want him back here, Mum!"

"Kerry, listen to me, he's sorry. And he's just having a bad day. He loves you, He is sobbing uncontrollably, I can see how much he loves you. Let him come back."

I sighed and put the phone down. Maybe I was overreacting.

So I did what she said. My love for George didn't disappear just because he'd lobbed a phone at my head. I was shocked and confused. But knowing he was sorry seemed to make it alright again – and my mum had fought his corner which at least meant he still had her seal of approval.

To be honest it's something I think about even now. I should've walked away the second I saw Molly crying and I struggle to forgive myself for that.

But even if I had left, I'm sure he would've found another way to persuade me back. And of course I can't sit here and act like a victim. I'm not. I do have to hold myself accountable because from that moment, subconsciously or not, I knew what I was getting into.

He came back to the house and apologised again. The way he did it, it was as if his love was oxygen. Seriously, having this 6ft 4 man, hard as nails with a criminal record sit down crying, begging for my forgiveness because he loves me so much – it was truly the most powerful thing. I've never felt that before and to me that was a huge turn on. From that moment he had me – hook, line and sinker – and life went on as if the attack had never happened in the first place.

We decided to move back up north. It made sense for us as it was where we were both from and to be honest at that point, I was done with living in Guildford. I could see my future with George back in familiar surroundings. By this point his temper had become more noticeable. He'd lash out but I wasn't particularly worried. I still felt I could change him and things would smooth themselves out. I ignored the few occasions he'd get aggressive or shout, because at this point the good truly did outweigh the bad. We'd still spend more time laughing than fighting and my feelings for him were only getting deeper, so walking away never seemed an option.

But things would get progressively worse.

Another early example of George's temper came when we went to view a house (we eventually settled, albeit temporarily, in Wigan) and the landlord was showing us around. In the living room there was a case of CDs and I happened to see a Bryan Adams album. Now I'd met Bryan once upon a time, I'd been to dinner with him and his partner when I was married to Brian McFadden. Brian was hoping to write with him, so we all met up, and I have to say, he was a lovely guy.

Anyway, in light of seeing this CD, I'm recounting the tale to George and the landlord, about my dinner with Bryan Adams, one of the biggest pop stars in the world and who, let the record show, was there with his own female companion.

I had this big plate of vegetables in front of me, and I didn't fancy them, but Bryan kept urging me in his fantastic Canadian drawl, "Eat them, you have to eat your greens!"

"...And then, Bryan Adams fed me broccoli off a fork!" I told George and this random landlord proudly, recalling the moment when yes, the rock god did just that.

"That's my claim to fame!"

There was nothing sexual or romantic about that moment with Bryan, it was just a jokey exchange between two people who had just met and were getting along well – in front of their significant others.

But clearly George didn't see it that way.

The atmosphere changed in a second. I saw his face fall, a shadow went across it and his eyes blazed.

Oh God.

We left the house viewing quickly, got in the car and as he drove off he had one hand on the steering wheel and one around my neck. He started to strangle me. I could barely breathe and honestly thought I was done for, when he released his grip, pulled over, opened the passenger side door and dragged me out of the car by my hair. I fell like a sack of spuds onto the pavement, hitting my head on the door as I tumbled. He spat on me and turned away, got back in the car and drove off, leaving me at the side of the road, breathless, red-faced, scared and embarrassed.

All because Bryan Adams had fed me broccoli off a fork.

I immediately found my way to my mum's, looking for some sort of comfort and safety. I should've known it would be the one place George would track me down.

In what seemed like the blink of an eye he was stood outside her house, screaming for me and threatening to kick her door down, which he did.

That was the first time Mum had seen what George was really like and I think in that moment she immediately regretted persuading me to take him back just a few weeks before.

She was terrified, she hadn't seen that kind of behaviour since her ex died. It must have brought back bad memories for her because she was truly shaken. She begged me to call the police but I told her not to because George was on probation. But her reaction frightened me.

This was a woman who had experienced the most awful violence imaginable at the hands of a man – she'd had a shotgun held to her head, for God's sake – so to see her react like this to George, I knew it was bad.

So many people wonder why I didn't just walk away once the abuse progressed. Well, in that particular instance I knew only going back to George, quietly, obediently, could dissolve the situation. Another reason I didn't want the police involved was I didn't want that kind of drama attached to me. I couldn't bear the press attention, especially after everything I'd been through with Mark Croft. Seeing as I was completely clean from drugs and had my shit sorted at that point, it was the last thing I needed.

Plus, as I've said before but can't stress enough: the bottom line is I was in love with him. And every time he was violent I thought it would be the last. I knew what I was getting into, I knew he'd beaten up women in the past and beaten up coppers, but, like all girls, I thought I could be the one to change him. I thought his love for me would be stronger than his temper.

It's only when you're so far in you can't see the wood for the trees and you realise you're in too deep to get out of the forest safely. Some time later, once we'd moved back down south yet again, I sent pictures of my two black eyes to my mum and told her: "If anything happens to me, if I'm found dead – this is why."

Years later she told me she used to anticipate the police knocking on the door, telling her I'd been killed.

And I can see why. George would fly off the handle over the most ridiculous things. And it left me so scared of him. One night I found the strength to kick him out, and hours later, when I was sleeping, he snuck back in and just watched me as I slept. How frightening is that?! Another time he threatened to rape and kill my mum during an argument.

He was so, so messed up.

*****

In late 2012 I started filming a show called The Big Reunion, with a load of bands from my era (ie, the early 00s) getting back together and putting on a show. It should have been a career resurgence for me, following the bad press I'd got thanks to the Mark Croft madness, so I was really, really looking forward to it. The show was broadcast on ITV2 and ended up being a huge ratings hit. Although I loved filming it, it coincided with the start of George getting really violent towards me, but of course you'd never know that watching it back. I was getting good at hiding things.

I was back with the Atomic Kitten girls, Liz McClarnon and Natasha Hamilton, and Blue, the boyband, were also on the bill. I've known those lads for years and years and to be honest they're all like my brothers. Especially Antony Costa, who's a great friend of mine and was throughout the entire time we were growing up in the industry.

He's seen and done it all too, bankruptcy, falling from grace, tabloid shame – he's like a male version of me! And, just like me, he's got a heart of gold too.

We'd be hanging out together during filming, a big group of us, and George would come along too, getting to know everyone and trying to fit in. It was becoming apparent at this point (although it was to get much worse later) that George wanted to be included in almost every aspect of my life, including my job.

We were all sitting there chatting one day and I went to sit on Costa's knee while we were filming a VT. I was having a laugh, playing the class clown and trying to entertain everyone. It was all completely innocent – Costa is like my brother.

# The Violence Begins

But when George saw me sitting there, laughing my head off, I knew I was in trouble.

It wasn't immediate. He was careful not to kick off in front of other people, especially a big cast like that, but once we made it back to our hotel that evening he went absolutely mental.

"You slag!" he screamed as he grabbed a fistful of my hair, which was cropped close to my head at the time. I could feel my skull burning.

"You disgusting slut," he raged at me. "You think you can make a fool out of me, do ya? Do ya?!"

I was sobbing at this point, still not entirely sure why me sitting with my mate had warranted this sort of reaction.

"Please George, you're hurting me! Please stop!"

He skull-dragged me across the room of the hotel where we were staying and locked me in the bathroom as punishment.

I slept in a bathtub that night, cold, alone, petrified.

The next day I had to go and film a scene for the show. The set-up was me and the other Kittens around a piano practising our song Whole Again. At this point the effects of the night before, the fear, the pain, the fact I ended up sleeping in a bloody bathroom, all started to get to me and I began to cry.

Go back and watch the scene, you'll probably find it on YouTube. What you see is Kerry Katona crying because she was, 'so moved by the whole experience, the reunion, the singing, the music'. The truth was I was in bits because I was so terrified of going back to that hotel room again once the cameras were off.

In my head I couldn't compute how I was there, surrounded by a production crew and fellow singers on this huge TV show, playing the part of a proper pop star, when the night before I was being pulled across a bathroom floor by my hair and made to sleep in a bath.

It was a particularly low point for me, but still, even at that moment, it didn't cross my mind to leave George. I was so far into the relationship, I couldn't imagine leaving it and enduring another break-up. I couldn't bear the drama, people's opinions, the attention that comes with it. Not after everything I'd been through up until that point.

I was frightened of him, yes, but don't get me wrong, I'd give as good as I got when the time called for it. I wasn't a victim by any means and even then I kept thinking, 'He must just be having a bad week, this isn't George.'

You have to remember, the violence wasn't every day or anything like that. At this point the incidents were terrifying but not regular. Most days, at this stage, George was still amazing and kind and charming, and I'd hold on to that. He wasn't a full time monster. Not yet.

It was seven months into our romance when he proposed to me on top of the Blackpool Tower. He'd roped the kids into it and the whole gang were there to witness me say, 'Yes!' without hesitation. What can I say? Maybe a small part of me thought once I was actually married to him the abuse would stop. Naive, I know but when you're conflicted – in love and in fear – you grasp on to whatever positive outcome you can muster up. Maybe getting hitched would calm him down, he'd see I was his fully and he didn't need to be jealous or over protective of me.

I actually thought we were going for dinner that night, so the proposal was a genuine surprise.

This was a man who told me he never wanted to get married. But yet….here he was, wanting to marry *me*.

# The Violence Begins

The space was decorated with roses and the champagne was on ice. I have to hand it to George, the whole thing was incredibly romantic. The hard man had a soft side too.

He got down on one knee while the kids giggled behind him.

"Kerry, I love you so much. Will you marry me?!"

For the first time in a long time the tears streaming down my face were ones of joy. In spite of it all, this was still the man I wanted forever.

"Yes!" I yelped. It was Molly who then handed me the white gold and diamond engagement ring. I looked in awe at the stunning piece of jewellery. The boy done good.

Still, despite how thrilled I was, when it came to me and George, nothing was ever straight forward. In this case my keenness to get married also stemmed from the fact an ex-girlfriend of his was back on the scene, and the thought of possibly losing him to her just made me want him even more. I wanted to get that ring on my finger so the bitch would back off! Everyone fancied George you see, and I loved the fact he was mine.

Of course he absolutely played off this – thrived on it in fact! He knew full well I'd be rushing things along while he made me believe this woman was trying to get him back. The jealousy was unlike anything I'd felt before! And he loved it.

Like I said, the toxic element of our relationship was starting to show very quickly.

But nevertheless I was overjoyed I'd got my man and I did start to think things would calm down. They certainly didn't *slow* down though. Instead, things were about to take a very interesting, blessed and slightly terrifying turn.

I fell pregnant.

# 3

DJ

It was just three months after the wedding proposal we found out I was expecting. We hadn't exactly been trying but we certainly weren't being careful, so we couldn't really call it a surprise.

I should've known full well I was pregnant as I hadn't felt right for a little while. The lack of energy, the nausea, all the signs were there.

Crunch time came one sunny day in early July, 2013. I was performing with Atomic Kitten, if I recall it was at one of the Big Reunion gigs. It turns out the TV show had been a huge success and the fans genuinely loved seeing all us oldies back together again so a string of concerts came off the back of it.

It was a lovely day, the crowd were on fine form and me and the girls were excited to be back doing what we loved.

But I couldn't shake this horrible feeling – as mums will know well, that early pregnancy fatigue can be a killer, though I hadn't put two and two together at the time.

Things came to a head when I nearly fainted backstage. I was massively struggling to breathe, to the point they put me on

28

oxygen. Of course I still hadn't worked it out and I put it down to a chest infection. The show carried on and I tried my best to get through the rest of the gig.

A few days later I had a couple of days off, and felt well enough to visit Chester Zoo with George and the kids. We had a lovely morning, seeing the animals, doing all the activities, and I was loving spending my time with the family, although I knew I wasn't one hundred per cent. I think we were looking at some penguins when I started to feel dizzy. Suddenly I could see stars.

The next thing I know, George was picking me up off the floor. I'd blacked out.

"That's it," he said. "We're getting you to the hospital."

I got up, dazed and confused and simply looked at him and nodded. Something wasn't right. Once at the local A&E, I did a urine sample and sure enough, we were told we were pregnant.

George and I stared at each other. I grinned, he grinned. Well, actually he was practically beaming. He was clearly over the moon. You see, George couldn't wait to get me pregnant. Most men can't, clearly! But I knew he wasn't trying to trap me, not like some fellas would. I was still in bankruptcy, so I knew it wasn't about money. Mind you, he did love the fame.

Despite his behaviour – the anger, the violence, I don't ever doubt he cared about me. Having a child together did come from a place of love and I still believe that to this day.

And we were so deeply in love. I still remember that feeling of sheer happiness when he came home one day, shortly after we found out about the baby, with a 'K' initial tattooed behind his ear. I reciprocated with a 'G' and even now I can't bring myself to cover it up or remove it. I could, and maybe I should, but I just don't want to, despite what the papers say.

Anyway, regardless of the rocky start, physically I ended up having the best pregnancy with DJ. She was by far the easiest one of all my kids. It was textbook.

I already had my Max, so I would've been happy for either gender but George was desperate for a boy, he didn't want a girl because he thought little girls were too much of a headache! Of course the second DJ arrived she was perfect– and continues to be – but in his mind it was a genuine risk.

Now in hindsight I wonder if I dodged a bullet by having a daughter. I think if we'd had a son I would've spent my life worrying he'd inherit all his dad's worst traits. The temper, the toxicity, the abuse. Would he have been as big and imposing as his dad? Would he have scared me?!

Mind you, I do worry sometimes about DJ now she's older. I get scared for her when she has temper tantrums that she can't seem to control, when she works herself up so much she can barely breathe. That's so George.

I'm not sure if her behaviour has something to do with his death, or if it stems from the things she witnessed when she was super tiny. I wonder sometimes if she was affected by what her daddy did even before she was born?

Because sadly George continued the violence even when our baby was in my belly.

It was bizarre to me, as normally dads are incredibly protective of the pregnant mums – or at least they should be – but George couldn't seem to control himself. Even as my stomach grew, he would push me over, kick me and spit in my face. But soon after he'd apologise, tell me how much he loved me and gently let me know it was all my fault because I pushed his buttons. And then I'd be the one apologising.

And at this point I've no doubt he was getting ever deeper into substance abuse too.

I'll never, ever forget when I was quite heavily pregnant, we had an electrician round. We'd bought a TV bed for the new house and he came over to fix it all up for us.

So George had gone out, and I was sat on the side of the bed, resting my feet and bump, while this electrician stood up next to the other side of the bed – literally metres away from me – playing with the remote. Next thing I know the door goes, I hear the sound of footsteps coming up the stairs and George walks in. Immediately I knew. I just knew. The energy in the room changed and I watched his face. I felt the shift straight away.

This poor electrician must have been in his sixties and yet he moved like a man half his age, hurrying out as George screamed at him to leave.

Then, when the 'leccy was out of the house, George turned his attention back to me. He took me by the throat and lifted me off my feet against the wardrobe.

"You think it's ok to be sat on our bed with another fucking man?!" he spat. "In my bedroom?!"

"He was showing me how to work the TV, George!" I pleaded.

"Don't fucking lie to me!" he yelled back, still gripping my throat two feet off the floor.

"George, please I can't breathe. Think of the baby, George! You could be hurting the baby!"

But he didn't care. He never did in the heat of the moment.

He continued to squeeze my neck before dropping me with a thud back to the floor. I was crouched in the foetal position, sobbing.

He spat at me again and walked out of the room. I could hear him murmuring the word 'slag' as he left, while I rocked myself back and forth, whimpering and praying the baby was ok.

Despite scenes like that, we were in a good place when DJ finally arrived on April 4, 2014 at the John Radcliffe Hospital in Oxford. I know people will read this and question why on earth I continued to stay in a relationship with a man like that, but as I said, when George wasn't being awful, he was the best. And when you're pregnant and your kids call him Daddy, it makes it hard to leave. Although to be honest, I didn't even want to. I was learning to accept that the violence was part of who George was. It was something I really believed I could live with at that point. Regardless of how much he'd kick or hit me while I was pregnant, I still thought he'd change once his daughter was here. The love he'd feel would surely stop him from allowing her to ever see him like that?!

I'd started getting contractions the night before and we got that nervous excitement that indicates a new life is about to come into the world. It was all systems go. I'd done this four times before, so I knew what I was doing and I just couldn't wait to meet my little baby. And I was so excited to give George that experience too. I couldn't wait for him to be a dad.

The contractions lasted for hours and by the time I'd been admitted to the labour ward, the pain was unbearable and I was begging for relief. I'd had epidurals with my other babies so I thought I'd be fine to have one this time as well, but on this occasion I really regretted it.

I was sat up on the bed, with George stood between my legs while I had my arms around him as they gave me the epidural. But unlike the others, this time didn't feel like relief. It felt like an out of body experience. I couldn't feel a thing, but I knew full well something wasn't right. I felt out of control and scared. I wasn't sure if I was working myself up, or if I just had that intuition (something that would serve me well in the years to come) but either way I started to freak out.

It was at this point a tiny, beautiful baby shot out of me. She literally came out as if she were on a water slide, it was that fast.

I was shocked, still numb from the epidural, relieved she was out, but still, I just knew in my heart something was wrong. Everything was a bizarre, super speedy, blur.

They quickly took our daughter, wrapped her in a blanket and counted her fingers and toes, while I started to feel pangs of pain resurfacing.

She had six fingers on each hand.

At this point George started crying. Not because he was upset by the genetic deformity, he was absolutely delighted by it. He too had been born with 12 fingers and he was so proud because he felt she was just like him. And she was, she was the image of her dad. Fingers and all. There was no denying that paternity!

But while George wept tears of joy, I was starting to feel tears of terror form in my eyes. By this point they'd handed the baby back to me, and I was holding her, gazing down at her, while the midwife was working on me. I still couldn't feel much, but apparently my placenta had got stuck and there was blood everywhere.

A shiver of fear came over me. As I looked at our little girl I just knew she wasn't well. I could feel myself choking with fright, my voice getting high and squeaky in panic.

"Something's not right," I wheezed, as weak as I was. "Please, something's not right with the baby! She's not breathing!"

I'd held her for all of twenty seconds before she was taken from me.

The midwife immediately pressed a button and a crash team came in and started doing chest compressions on our daughter. George, whose tears of happiness were now replaced by wide eyes filled with fear, was trying to stop me from looking in all the panic, but by this point I was borderline hysterical. And I was getting weaker. My placenta had ruptured inside of me, which is actually a leading cause of death in childbirth. There was every chance both me and my baby could die.

A cart came over to fetch me as it suddenly became clear I'd need emergency surgery. But George being George took it upon himself to lift me up and carry me to the theatre himself, kicking through the door as he went like some sort of bargain bin George Clooney in ER.

You see, the doctors had given him a choice. Go with your partner, or stay with the baby.

George had looked at DJ and back at me.

"I'm staying with Kerry."

"No, George, stay with the baby, it's ok," I said. Knowing what an impossible decision it was for him.

"No," he said, now allowing the tears to flow again. "I don't even know that baby. I'm sticking with you."

I truly believe the guilt of that decision messed his head up massively. I don't think he ever forgave himself for that.

But still, he came with me. And I'm there, being sick all over him, now in agonising pain that not even the remains of the epidural could touch, and drifting in and out of consciousness as the doctors battled to save my life, while another team worked on our tiny daughter in a different room.

# DJ

Of course, I survived. But only just. Following my surgery, where they had to scrape my placenta from my body because it wouldn't shift naturally, I was put in a recovery room where I could hear all these little babies crying, still unsure what would become of mine.

"You have to give your baby a name," the midwife told me, looking like she was fighting back tears herself. "Name her, Kerry. We don't think she'll make it through the night."

For all the pain, abuse and heartache I'd witnessed in my life, I can safely say that was the most horrendous moment of my entire existence.

"Please," I wept. "Please save my baby."

We opted to name the child Dylan-Jorge Rose, DJ for short.

It turns out DJ had something wrong with a valve in her heart. It was to do with a chamber opening the wrong way. Obviously she came through it and they fixed the problem, but she was on life support for four days.

I was ill for longer, expressing milk for the baby, which was like gold dust to her, and once she was fixed up, she was right as rain. It took me a lot longer to recover, both emotionally and physically.

Soon after I asked George how he'd felt about the whole debacle.

"I honestly thought you were going to die," he told me. "And I wondered who the hell would pay the rent."

\*\*\*\*\*

I know the experience has had such a profound effect on me, it's the reason I can't go through with another pregnancy. I want to freeze my eggs so that I have the option of a surrogate at some point, because I can't put myself through that again. As much as I want to give my now fiancé Ryan a child of his own, I can't risk my existing children losing their mum. I would sometimes wonder if the violence I suffered while pregnant might have played a part in the traumatic birth, but I'm afraid in my case it was all just bad luck. And it's something I just can't risk again.

After DJ was born, I really believe I had Post Traumatic Stress Disorder. In fact, it was one of the reasons I started drinking around that time – that and the continuing abuse from George and his controlling manner.

I was struggling a lot with the fact I nearly lost my life and DJ nearly lost hers. I started downing up to three bottles of Prosecco a day, although I remained super cautious of not letting the kids see me drunk.

But it wasn't just the guilt I felt over DJ's first, stressful few days on earth that was causing me to struggle. Even though I was a new mum with four other kids, I felt like I didn't have a purpose, because George was doing everything. He never left my side.

He took control of the feeds, the school run, the shopping, the cooking. To most women that sounds like a dream scenario, but it wasn't, I felt completely redundant. I'd lost my independence entirely and because I was drinking so much as a result of that, it gave him a reason to call me an alcoholic and a bad mother.

And George loved having that power over me. That's why he'd come home from the shops sometimes with the bottles. I didn't even want them, but he'd make sure they were there so I drank them. I was powerless really, I'd drink the booze he bought me, only for him to give out to me because I was drinking it.

# DJ

At this point he was a nightmare. When he wasn't controlling every last element of our home life, he was now obviously taking a lot of cocaine. I know this because the drugs made him crazy. His mental health would be dreadful when he was on a bender but I was powerless to stop him.

I genuinely don't know why he put that stuff in his body when it clearly didn't agree with him. It didn't make him happy, or giddy, and as one who has taken a lot of coke in my day, I'd say that's the only reason you would want it. For the release, to stop the pain. Not make it worse.

When DJ was three months old George was sectioned under the Mental Health Act, after he was found running down the street screaming that someone was going to kill him. According to people there he was darting and in and out of cars, yelling and threatening no one in particular.

I was both mortified and terrified – I really didn't want this sort of press following me and I was also scared for George and what he was going through. How can this even be happening when we have a new baby in the house?!

The police released a statement after a woman called for help. At the time another neighbour was quick to talk to the papers about it.

"He was behaving very strangely – actually it was quite frightening," the old busybody told the salivating press.

"A woman who was driving down the road was so upset by what he was doing that she stopped and dialled 999 for the police!"

*Great.*

George was released soon after and no further action was taken, but it was a big fright for all of us. It turns out that during this episode of his, he'd suffered the equivalent of three heart attacks and later admitted to mixing steroids and sleeping pills with alcohol. I couldn't believe this was happening.

Afterwards we went into damage control mode and he gave an interview to the press in which he said, "I'm heartbroken I've put Kerry through this. The brain is so delicate and the doctors said it was a chemical imbalance. I had no feeling of madness or that I was going to cause absolute uproar and rampage down the street."

Of course I knew there was more to it, but I played along to keep the peace.

I was used to seeing George play the hard man, so to witness him in such a vulnerable position – for the first time in what would turn into many times – was harrowing to say the least. But a part of me felt nurturing towards him. I wanted to look after him. I wanted to protect him. That was how messed up this was all becoming.

We tried our best to put the incident behind us and when George was sober he went back to being the tough guy. He never seemed to hurt me when he was on drugs, he'd hurt himself. But when he was sober, it was me who'd take the brunt of whatever problems he'd conjure up in his head. It was exhausting.

Despite my hope that a baby would change things, it seemed to make him even more controlling and reckless. The mind games never stopped.

And maybe that's why I never stopped the wedding. Of all the things in my life I had suddenly lost control of, I was still 'allowed' to start sorting plans for our big day.

Organising that actually gave me a purpose and so, with a sense of impending doom, that's exactly what I did.

# 4

# I Do, Again

I've been married twice before so I was already a dab hand at weddings by this point.

My first, to Brian, was a genuine fairytale. It was 2002's showbiz event of the year and so many famous guests of the time were there, including all of Westlife, the Atomic Kitten girls and Dane Bowers. I mean, it's not exactly William and Kate levels of grandeur, but these guys were the cream of the pop crop at the time, so don't underestimate what a big deal it was!

We spent hundreds of thousands of pounds on the day, it was covered in a national magazine and I felt like a princess as I held baby Molly in my arms while wearing my big white dress.

Perfect wedding, imperfect marriage.

And then there was Mark Croft. Two weeks before we got hitched at Gretna Green, he sprung it on me. It was something he'd planned in advance as a surprise, but the press got wind of it so he ended up telling me. He decided on an altogether more low key ceremony initially – I was heavily pregnant with Heidi and we said our vows quickly on Valentine's Day in 2007, with just six people there.

We were given some cash to cover it all with OK! magazine, including the bigger 'official' ceremony at Lake d'Orta in Italy, seven months later, once Heidi was born. The now disgraced – and dead – PR guru Max Clifford walked me down the aisle and about 50 of our friends and family were there. It wasn't nearly as 'showbiz' as mine and Brian's do, and of course the marriage itself was anything but glamorous.

Small wedding, big mistake.

It was difficult to know what road to take with mine and George's day. Would I go totally over the top again, like I did in 2002? Or keep it a bit more simple like the great Gretna Green ceremony of 2007?

I decided, probably because I was feeling so miserable, that I needed something to celebrate. I wanted to go all out. And it turns out George was more than up for that too.

"Do whatever makes you happy, Kerry," he'd say. As if I had that luxury usually.

We'd have OK! cover it again, I'd have a proper celebrity guestlist, which would make sense considering Atomic Kitten were flying high once more off the back of the Big Reunion. And all five kids would be there, so they could play a big role on the day, which was really important to me.

Although after DJ's birth I felt like I was spiralling, thanks to the guilt, the drinking, George's mental health crisis and the abuse, planning this wedding was providing the anchor I needed to keep me sane. We set the date for 14 September 2014.

My previous weddings felt like a lifetime ago, but yet still, those same feelings of doubt and panic were there. I pushed them to the back of my mind. OK, so having a baby didn't change George. But marriage? Marriage definitely would!

By this point even I knew I was lying to myself.

I invited Katie Price, Liz McClarnon and Danielle Brown to be my bridesmaids, alongside Lilly and Molly, while Heidi and DJ would be little flower girls. Karen Belton, a friend of mine for years, was maid of honour. Antony Costa and Scott Robinson from boyband 5ive would be groomsmen and Max would be part of George's gang too. We would rely on the magazine money to cover the costs, so that we could go all out without feeling guilty and I'd get myself the most stunning wedding dress I could afford, which I did. A strapless fishtail gown by Morilee that made me feel a million dollars.

I was going to do anything and everything to make myself feel good about this marriage. I even booked the Tortworth Court Four Pillars Hotel, in Gloucestershire, a really stunning Grade II listed manor house, which just screamed class and money.

"Oh George, it looks so beautiful", I'd say, dreamily, as I looked over the brochure with him. "It's perfect."

Clearly putting my wedding to Brian to the back of my head, I'd convinced myself that a beautiful ceremony would mean a beautiful marriage. I obviously hadn't learnt my lesson there.

With wedding prep in full swing it also fell to me to organise our joint hen and stag dos. Let's face it, there was no way in hell George was gonna let me have a party with the girls without him there. What could well have been seen as a super romantic 'double celebration' was actually a means of him keeping an eye on me. A ladies-only hen party wasn't an option for me. He made that very clear.

But ultimately it was an amicable decision, simply because I was still so messed up from when Brian cheated on me during his stag. Trust me, I was very happy to keep an eye on George too.

And besides, it would be fun! A joint stag and hen do. A sten!

We organised a day at a hotel in South London that August, with OK! magazine in tow. We had about thirty people there, half George's lot, half mine. We had sorted spa treatments and drinks and dinner and then we'd arranged for a boat trip across the Thames with everyone. A sort of luxury London cruise, which felt like something a bit different, a bit special.

Well the party was special alright, but for all the wrong reasons.

Throughout the day, I sat with the girls, drinking Prosecco and having a giggle, while George and his boys did their own thing. We'd enjoyed some joint spa treatments earlier, but in terms of being together constantly? Well so far, this was not the imposing, overwhelming George-not-leaving-my-side shindig I had been expecting. Instead things felt quite chilled, though I was still on edge. It was hard not to be when it came to George. And because OK! was there, I was desperate for everything to go well. I couldn't bear the thought of him kicking off.

But I don't really recall seeing him at all for the majority of the day. Despite deep down being a nervous wreck, I became engrossed in girl talk, loving the feeling of being able to speak (fairly) freely with my besties, knowing George was somewhere nearby but not interfering.

But of course I should've known such peace wouldn't last.

I had asked him – no, *begged* him – not to do drugs that day. But George being George, he couldn't help himself. When he finally joined me, God knows how long after I'd last seen him, he was high as a kite. He wasn't quite at the point of paranoia, although that was to come, but he was on one.

I had gone back to my hotel room to freshen up before we were due to board the boat that evening. My manager at the time, Paul, had come with me, just to chat over a few things. No doubt the paps were about so he was probably briefing me on that.

George came into the room and I could tell he was high. He immediately went for Paul, threatening to beat him up, getting so close to Paul's face there was spittle on his skin. Paul, who was a wet blanket anyway, cowered in the corner, shaking with fear.

"I haven't seen you all day!" George bellowed at me. "This was supposed to be a joint party, what the hell happened?!"

This was classic George, using reverse psychology on me as a means of beating me down.

"You've been with your boys, doing God knows what," I yelled back, fuelled by the adrenaline of the moment and genuinely annoyed he was kicking off when HE was the one who'd gone off to do his own thing.

"Don't backchat me Kerry," he warned. "I've not seen you for hours and you're here being mouthy to me?! Who do you think you are?!"

"Oh get over yourself," I screamed back. I was sure with Paul still there and the fact I was standing up for myself, George wouldn't physically attack me.

He was fuming, but I was equally enraged. How dare he come up like this and have a go at me? On my hen night?

It caused such a commotion and it led us to have one almighty row. It was then that George did the right thing and left before things got even nastier. He just legged it. I later found out he'd gathered a few of the lads together and they went off clubbing, leaving a boatful of guests scratching their heads as they waited to set sail.

I was heartbroken. I was humiliated and embarrassed and the fact that all my friends and family – and OK! Magazine – were there to see us fight like that was mortifying. I couldn't physically believe he'd bailed like that. I couldn't get my head around it. He'd just upped and left, without a second thought for anyone who'd come all that way to celebrate with us.

Everyone on board was told to go home. The cruise was off. The papers got wind of the debacle thanks to a 'source' selling their story and claiming it was all a 'disaster'. Well they weren't wrong. It *was* a bloody disaster.

I was in tears at the way everything had transpired. Later that night, as I sat in that hotel room all by myself, wondering what the hell he was up to, ringing him constantly and seeing pictures on his Instagram of him off his head in a nightclub with his mates and some woman, I just kept praying the wedding wouldn't go the same way. George was so, so unpredictable and to see a lovely day with friends turn into something truly awful just because he had the hump was so disappointing. Why couldn't he just behave like a normal human being?!

He didn't come back to the hotel that night, which only enraged me more. It's not like I even wanted to see him, but I fully expected him to apologise and acknowledge the fact we'd left a load of our good mates stranded and confused on the banks of the Thames.

I wasn't going to take it lying down.

# I Do, Again

I woke up the next morning and knowing he wasn't there, went to the wardrobe and pulled out his clothes. I stuck them in the bathtub, filled it with water and left them to soak.

It wasn't quite the same punishment he'd dish out to me, but in my own little way, I felt a hell of a lot better just knowing the inconvenience it would cause him.

I got in the car and went up north with my mum, back to hers.

It was then that George's mum rang me, wanting to know what the hell had happened – and that's when she begged me not to marry him.

Now, this whole situation is a prime example of fate stepping in for the better. Of something that was always meant to be. Because even though I was devastated from the night before, I thank God things transpired the way they did and I was able to make that trip to Warrington. I definitely wouldn't have gone if the party had continued as planned. But it ended up being the last time I ever saw my nan alive, the woman who basically raised me.

As soon as George found out I was at my mum's, he followed me up there, as he always did. Once he found me he made me get in the car to go back down south – but before I left I asked him if we could pop in to see my nan because I knew she wasn't feeling too well.

George drove me round the corner from my mum's to my nan's with little DJ. When I got inside it was the strangest feeling. It took me right back to my childhood. My Aunty Angela was there, so was her husband Lenny and her two children – none of us had been in the same room together for God knows how long. Families, eh?

I sat with my nan at the kitchen table. She was 84, she was smoking a Lambert and Butler but she just wasn't herself. She was confused. She was convinced it was the first time she'd met DJ, but it wasn't. I put DJ on her knee and took a picture.

I spoke to her about the wedding.

"Cancel it, Kerry," she told me.

"Cancel what?" I asked.

"The wedding. Leave it for six months at least."

I thought it was a strange thing to say, but in hindsight, she must have had a sixth sense about it. She was urging me not to go through with it.

It was the last thing she ever said to me.

I gave her a kiss and said goodbye. We left the house and got in the car.

I turned to George. "That's the last time I'm going to see my nan alive," I said.

"Don't be silly," he replied. "You'll see her next week when you're up here again."

We got back down south about midnight, then at six in the morning our Angela texted me with the awful news. Nan had died.

I fell on the floor screaming, crying – completely inconsolable. To think, I'd taken that one last picture of her, said my goodbyes and the next day she was gone.

If I hadn't had that argument with George on the boat and gone back home with my mum, I would never have seen my nan again. So thank heavens for small blessings.

For all his faults, George also had this amazing softer side, and when my Nan died he really stepped up for me. It was a huge distraction from what had gone down at the Sten party.

Suddenly we weren't focused on that debacle, but rather on the tragedy of losing someone so special. He was loving and understanding. Plus he was just as devastated as me. He loved my nan. He was one of her pallbearers.

In fact it was at her wake where we chose the song we had our first dance to. We slow danced to 'Drift Away' by Dobie Gray, and it gave me butterflies. We had a slow, loving snog and it was a beautiful moment. Having that song at our wedding felt like our tribute to my nan.

So, with my nan's death taking up a lot of our thoughts, we got over the Sten madness pretty quickly. It was certainly embarrassing to have that sort of press attention but the fact remains – it *was* a shit show. It was a horrible experience and I was truly sorry to my lovely friends who must've been fuming that the night ended the way it did.

But this was the norm for me now, putting George and his drama above anyone else, including myself. So life just went back to the regular swing of things.

I had the wedding to focus on and I just kept praying it would go smoothly. We had a mag deal, so it *had* to go well. There's no way I'd get paid if anything went tits up. I can't imagine the magazine hitting the shelves the following week with my big beaming face on the front if, in fact, the whole thing had been a disaster. No doubt the tabloids would have a field day at my expense, though. Everything had to go to plan.

It turns out the wedding was absolutely brilliant, for the most part. Probably the favourite of mine, in fact! Thank God.

We had so much fun but little did I know George wanted to do a runner the night before! His mate told me he'd wanted to get in a helicopter, fly to Cape Verde of all places and do one.

To this day I don't know why, although he had been up all night the evening before, so who knows, maybe it was drugs talking? Maybe the nerves got to him? Either way, I was upset when I found out, but I kept my mouth shut and got over it – and he got himself down the aisle.

The morning wasn't without its issues. Katie Price was supposed to be a bridesmaid but she pulled out as I was getting ready. She still came to the wedding, she just wasn't part of the bridal party. I can't remember now what the issue was, something about her dress not being right I think. She'd just had her daughter Bunny though, and that was probably part of the reason. I wasn't best pleased. I was probably a bit of a bridezilla anyway, so I felt pretty pissed off, but Danielle sat me down and gave me the pep talk I needed.

The ceremony itself went without a hitch. Little Max walked me down the aisle to the Shania Twain song "You're Still The One" and I remember just staring at George and thinking how fit he looked. Nothing ever stopped me fancying him. No amount of rows or abuse. Whenever I looked at him, especially then in his tux, my knees would go to jelly and I'd remind myself how lucky I was to have such a gorgeous man want me.

Scott and Danielle read some nice speeches and mine and George's vows were really lovely too. I thought he did a great job, which only romanticised everything all the more.

I can still recall it now. He looked at me, smiled and said:

*"You bring laughter, fun and light into my life. You are a beautiful person inside and out. It will be a privilege to care for you and also to stand by your side through whatever life may throw at us."*

My heart was racing with love. I replied:

# I Do, Again

*"My whole life I've always felt a little lost. I've always tried to find the missing piece but nothing ever worked until I met you. Now I don't feel lost. I've been found by my prince and found by the most wonderful daddy to my children."*

In that moment – in spite of everything that had happened since the second we reconnected at that bar on my birthday two years before – I meant every word.

As I went to wipe a tear away, I turned around and surveyed the guests, hoping they felt as happy for me as I felt for myself in that second. My beloved Danielle was practically sobbing, the old softie. Natasha Hamilton was bawling her eyes out!

Looking around at the room full of faces of the people who had thankfully forgiven us for the Sten debacle, I felt so lucky and grateful. Partly out of relief that this wedding was going my way and partly because I truly did feel so loved in those moments.

Our Molly had been due to sing the Leonard Cohen song 'Hallelujah' after we'd said our vows. She's always had a beautiful voice and I was excited for her to have her moment too.

But even though she started, and it sounded gorgeous, she quickly became overwhelmed and had to stop. George and I rushed to her side to console her – she really was so, so nervous, bless her, and was shaking like a leaf – so I thought I'd pipe up with a bit of humour to break the tension.

"I can do Whole Again instead?" I told the guests, who in turn collectively cackled with laughter. Of course I was joking but maybe I should have been offended that everyone found the prospect so amusing! I know I'm a singer and all but my voice has nothing on Molly's.

The reception that followed had it all, a contortionist,

49

a juggler and we opened champagne by way of a sword, which seems a little bit OTT in hindsight, and possibly a tad dangerous considering George's habit of suddenly switching from gentleman to psycho. But it was all in good fun and made for a terrific spectacle.

When it came to the speeches my memory does get a little hazy, no doubt because of the champagne we were all drinking, but a few zingers stick out in my mind.

George's brother telling the crowd he was made up for us as he'd always thought George was gay got a big laugh. The stories he and best man Richard shared about writing off three cars and George accidentally ripping the head off a chicken who was trapped in a fence when he pulled too hard, though, not so much.

In fact Richard took it one step further by actually making light of the problems George had faced that year. It was a smart move really, as it addressed the elephant in the room, but it was still shocking.

He gave me a parcel with a note on the front. I read the note out loud to the room full of guests digesting their sirloin steak.

*"Dear Miss Katona, please could you make sure George wears this straightjacket the next time he goes on one of his drink and steroid benders. Many thanks, Chief Inspector Smith, West Wycombe Police Force."*

Huge laughter followed from the crowd, and although I giggled my head off at the time, I recall that strange sensation in the pit of my stomach. 'It's not even a joke though, is it?' I thought to myself, before allowing the feeling to pass with another gulp of champagne.

It was then Lilly's turn to do her speech and a little poem.

She's always been the most confident of my lot and even now shows the most promise to follow me into the murky world of showbiz. She just has a natural talent for getting up in front of people and charming them.

The wedding was no different. She stole the show. She was funny, charismatic, and confident. I could've burst with pride.

"When I found out George was going to be my stepdad, my initial reaction was, 'Oh,'" she joked. (At least I think she was joking. Looking back now, maybe she really did think that.)

She continued. "George is family and we all love him" and concluded her little speech by saying, "I want my mum and stepdad to know that no matter what, me Molly, Max, Heidi and Dylan will always love them and remember all the great times and now we are all prepared to create new memories."

For an eleven year old, it was quite something. And for George, it was a hard act to follow.

His speech was as expected, romantic, sweet, but one part was particularly telling.

"I love you to bits," he said. "Thank you for putting up with my shit."

I couldn't help myself.

"That's an understatement", I roared as the guests cheered.

Oh how we were making light of something that was all too painfully real.

Unlike our Lilly, George was easily embarrassed in front of crowds and I know standing there, saying vows and speeches was an ordeal for him.

He was never one for attention in a group of people. For our slow dance he got quite panicked at the idea of everyone looking at him and had to clutch onto me.

He whispered in my ear, "Don't you leave me, don't walk away, stay right here".

It's so strange with George because he loved the fame that came from his association with me, but stick him in front of a crowd and he'd be like a scared child.

The rest of the evening did go smoothly though, bar Tash Hamilton being taken to hospital when they thought she might have gone into early labour. Her daughter, Ella Rose, did end up holding out another week before she made her proper entrance into the world. Also our Angela falling over on the dance floor and breaking her hand wasn't ideal, that was a bit of extra drama thrown into the mix.

But for me it was a wonderful day and I don't regret a second of it now, regardless of how our lives panned out later. My only real sadness is my nan wasn't there to see it.

I made sure she was there in spirit by having a tiny little angel sewn into my wedding dress at the last minute, by my heart. It was my way of honouring her memory.

It was so hard losing her and I know she'd have been happy for me on the day – but deep down I know she didn't want me to marry George.

So I guess no matter how much I missed her then and still do now, in a lot of ways it was a good thing she wasn't around to see how the marriage ended up.

I've no doubt she would have been as horrified as me.

# 5

# The Kids Aren't Alright

Things ticked along normally for a while as we settled into married life as a family of seven. But of course, as anyone reading this will have predicted from the start, if I'd thought for a second the abuse would stop once we were man and wife, I was very much mistaken.

Instead, the couple of years that followed turned out to be the worst of my life, as George became increasingly dependent on drugs, and his psychosis worsened, bringing us all to our knees.

I look back at this time with a mixture of relief and guilt. Relief that I managed to eventually get out, and guilt over the effect it had on the kids.

It was very, very rare that they'd actually witness any violence, I was incredibly mindful of that. But they heard the screaming, and they saw the black eyes, despite my efforts to cover them up with make-up.

I remember at the time I wouldn't acknowledge what was happening with them. And they wouldn't talk about it. We just brushed it under the carpet. I now know why I did that. I felt such terrible shame as a parent that I was letting my kids down, that I tried to ignore it. I blocked it out and tried to make myself believe they weren't suffering. How could they be, when my childhood was so much more traumatic? This is nowhere near as bad as what I went through!

Of course the reality is, everything is relative. This was their experience and it was equally as awful for them as my childhood had been for me and I had no right to take that away from them.

Even now, writing this, my stomach is in knots with the guilt of thinking how scared they must have been every time George raised his voice, or their terror as they heard their mum cry. I'm so aware of it now. It makes me feel like such a failure.

They are great kids now and everyone who meets them tells me what a credit they are to me, but in that period, which was so crucial in their development, I messed up. I ignored their pain. And I don't think many parents would admit that.

You see, I can't throw all the blame on George – I was responsible for staying with him. I was their mother and I allowed him to treat me like that. I know people will find that hard to hear, knowing how difficult it is for abused women to leave bad relationships, but even now I believe I should have known better and I should have found a way to leave.

And sometimes, I did find a way.

It was around this time we started splitting up and getting back together quite a lot. It was incredibly unhealthy and there was little stability for the kids, but I'd somehow find the strength to kick him out on different occasions. I'd have a few days – even weeks, sometimes, of respite – but we'd always end up back in bed and then we'd give things another go. Everything would be rosy for a while, and then it would all kick off again. He would smack me around the face when he got angry, but rather than apologise he'd say, "Happy now? Happy you got the black eye? You pushed me into that!"

He'd say I was like a red rag to a bull and that I should know better for pushing his buttons.

But I was starting to get bolder when it came to calling the police on George. After one particularly nasty row I got them out when his episodes were becoming too much. He was getting off his head most nights on coke and his paranoia was reaching new levels. It was so frightening to see him like that, getting the law onto him felt like the only way to keep our family safe.

They would look at it as a domestic disturbance, give us warnings, speak to me, who would inevitably back down, and then it would all go back to the start.

Statistics show that on average it takes 50 incidents for an abused woman to leave the relationship – and I'm living proof of that.

George would frequently go back to his parents around this time and the press were starting to pick up on our problems. We were bickering and broke, thanks to my previous bankruptcy issues. It wasn't a happy union.

In May 2015, after one of our many break-ups, he gave an interview to a magazine.

"It's been tough lately, we've been rowing a lot," he said. "Marriage isn't what I thought it would be if I'm honest. I thought it would be all sunshine and happiness, but it's really hard work – especially for us. We argue a lot over money issues. We have to live within a strict budget and that's tough. We're both fiery characters, too, so that doesn't help things."

He was right about that.

In the article he continued, "There have been times I've thought we might not last. In my darkest moments I've wondered if we should be together. But I love Kerry so much and I'm determined to make it work."

True to his word, he would come back, though it wouldn't be long before there was another incident and I'd be kicking him out again.

For the kids, this must have been a rough time and I often think back on them all as individuals, with their separate little personalities and wonder how they coped.

Molly wasn't the biggest fan of George at the start, but by the time we were married she was calling him dad. Even her actual father, Brian, accepted that and thanked George for being there. And George would honestly take a bullet for that girl.

When he was being 'good George', he adored her. But when he was on one, he could be terribly cruel to Molly. He'd call her crude names and belittle her. Her self esteem must have been so low and yet I kept brushing it off as banter, trying not to make a big deal out of it.

Of course it *was* a big deal to a young teenager and although I never saw her cry, I do worry that she spent most of her days in her room, alone, thinking about it and being upset by it. And I know full well she'd hear the shouting, just like she did that first time he threw the phone at my head. I should have done more to protect her, to protect all of them, and that's something I'll never get over. I am their mother. I take full responsibility for what they went through. It was my job to protect them and I didn't.

Molly and Lilly were teens before they ever saw me drunk,

which may surprise people. They never, ever saw me on drugs when I was with Mark Croft (though they'd hear me slurring, which, let me make very clear, was due to my bipolar medication).

I tried to keep that all well hidden from them. But they did hear the violence George inflicted on me. And to this day that gives me such terrible guilt. They'd never witnessed anything like that growing up and as a result I know Molly in particular is super protective of me now. It took her a long, long time to warm up to Ryan when he came on the scene.

Lilly, on the other hand, is a lot more easy going in that respect. Although I've had some issues with her as she got older, which I'll get to, around that time with George she remained calm and patient and, despite what was going on, she idolised him.

I know she was George's favourite too. They were as thick as thieves when he was on form and when he wasn't she was still quick to forgive him. Kids are so resilient anyway, they just accept their circumstances and get on with things.

She did keep a diary though, in which she wrote about some of the things she'd heard and how they'd upset her. I know he shouldn't have, but George read it. And it made him cry his eyes out.

He felt so guilty he immediately went out and bought Molly and Lilly a puppy each to try and make up for what he'd done.

You see, these were the two sides to George. He was so easy to forgive at times because he would be so loving and generous. But he'd turn.

The puppies didn't last long, incidentally. The girls just didn't look after them properly and, in what I still consider an instance of excellent parenting from George and I, we decided to give them away to a police unit – drug protection officers, ironically.

Molly and Lilly were absolutely devastated – crying, screaming blue murder, but I stand by that decision. We warned them so many times that if they wanted to keep the dogs, they'd have to be responsible for them. Were they heck. They left it all up to me, and it wasn't a hard decision for the dogs to go somewhere else. It was one of very few times around that period when Lilly wasn't having me. Usually she was my best friend.

I remember once, after taking a particularly bad beating and staying on the sofa overnight, I woke up to find her there, stroking my hair. She had some concealer with her and gently put it on my bruises, to cover them, without saying a word.

Make-up became my best friend at that point, which is saying something as I'd usually never wear it around the house. Sometimes I'd have to plaster it on so thick the kids would ask me why I was so glammed up.

"Are you going to a party, mummy?" Max would ask. Sadly, I wasn't going anywhere. I just couldn't bear for them to see the marks George had left on me.

Meanwhile, Max used to be so scared of George. But it wasn't because George would turn his anger on Max and try to hurt him. Max suffers from undiagnosed Aspergers Syndrome, which is something I'm still trying to educate myself on. Communication is difficult for him, he lashes out when he's frustrated and can be very aggressive, he has been ever since he was little and was a nightmare to control long before George came on the scene. He's always been unique.

As George became the man of the house, he would administer discipline to Max when needed. Not violence, but he'd tell him off to try and get Max to toe the line. But the little devil would go into the school the next day and tell the teachers all sorts. That George had slammed his hand in the door and starved him, which simply wasn't true. In fact, that was something that had stayed in Max's head from the Mark Croft days. Mark's daughter Keeley had been living with us. She'd swiped something from her dad and to punish her Mark threatened to shut her fingers in the door – of course he never did – but it was something Max heard us talk about after and I swear that's where he got his 'inspiration' for the tall tale from!

A few days later we'd get a call from the school saying Max had accused a dinner lady of hitting him, again a load of lies. At least they could see my point of view when it came to his porkies.

There were endless fibs and it was hard to keep track of it all. He would steal from us too, which, when you're a young kid, is quite a feat. He once nicked £250 that I'd had in my purse. I had to set up a sting operation on my mobile phone so I could film him in the act. Imagine that, when you're a little boy, having your mum do that just so she wasn't out of pocket. He was only six! Where the bloody hell did he think he'd spend that? Toys R Us?! He had an obsession with money even at that age. It's all part of his condition.

We've turned a corner with Max since Ryan came on the scene, but those days were terribly difficult. He's just always been a tricky little lad and I've always had to keep an eye on him as a result. I suppose being in the house with George made things worse, though at the time I felt like he needed that strong, male figure in his life.

But let's not get it wrong – George could be cruel to Max.

He used to call Molly and Lilly 'The Golden Girls' because they were Brian's daughters and then he'd refer to Max and Heidi as 'The druggie's kids'. I hated it. It's like he knew the kids were my weak spot and he'd use them against me. He'd throw my past in my face, knowing it would devastate me.

There were a couple of times that Max did see George be rough with me, although I always tried to diffuse the situation quickly.

George and I had been in the car with DJ, when was still little and in her car seat in the back. Something was obviously said, voices were raised and things escalated. When we parked up back at home, I went to unstrap DJ and George got me in a chokehold, pinning me to the back seat of the car, my back arching over DJ. He was squeezing my throat so tightly I thought I was going to pass out, when he suddenly let me go, spat on me and retreated from the vehicle.

As I got up and took DJ in my arms, I looked up at my house and I saw Max in the window watching it all. I don't think he saw much, only the tussle and the back of heads, and he didn't say anything. Nor did I. Again, I just brushed it under the carpet and thought 'it's not that bad, Kerry. It's really not that bad.'

Another time, I think it was Christmas if I recall, George had me on my knees, holding my hands up above my head in our bedroom. And Max came in. I could see the fright in his face.

"It's alright, Max. Get yourself in the other room, we're just playing. Everything's ok!" I told him as tears sprung to my eyes.

But George was on one and had other ideas. "Max, your mum's trying to kill me!" he shouted. Max must've been so confused to witness this bizarre situation, but again, it wasn't something we talked about. Although we've since been very open about our situation, I do believe that all the children need some kind of counselling as a result of the things they witnessed, and this is something I will never ever be able to forgive myself for.

Meanwhile, Heidi was similar in that she never spoke about the shouting she heard. And she really did adore George. That's what made it so hard to walk away. When he was good, he was brilliant. We all strived to make him happy, we craved those moments when he was on form. We lived for his approval.

And Heidi, who has always had daddy issues since Mark walked out on her, would be more like Lilly. She'd keep her head down and wait for the shouting to stop. Then, once the storm had passed she'd retreat back to George for cuddles and comfort. I couldn't bear the thought of another man letting her down, so I always breathed a sigh of relief when I saw her be affectionate with him. I tried hard not to make an issue of the times he was cruel to her too, be it calling her names or getting irritated with her. Again, ignore the problem and just wait for everything to be hunky dory again.

Honestly, as I sit here writing this, admitting to myself how I just ignored what was happening, it literally kills me inside. I know what an awful parent I've been in a lot of ways, and it breaks my heart for my kids.

But it was DJ who worried me the most around this time. She was picking up on things she'd seen her father do and even though she was still tiny, only just becoming a toddler really, she had started to spit on me.

It was so hard not to lose my temper when she did that, but I needed to understand why it was happening. She would punch and kick at me, lashing out when she got frustrated. It was all mimicked behaviour. It's almost impossible to tell a child not to do something when they see an adult do exactly the same. How do you tell a toddler, "Do as I say, not what I do?"

George didn't seem to see it as a problem – perhaps in some warped way he was secretly proud he'd had a child so similar to himself. But I knew in my heart that wasn't who DJ was. She was – and is – the sweetest, kindest, most gentle little girl you could wish to meet. She didn't know what she was doing. She had no concept of right or wrong.

In between the black eyes, DJ's spitting, Max's lies and the puppy debacle, George and I split again. This time I packed up the kids and moved to Crowborough, a town in East Sussex, into a rented house with plenty of space for what I thought was a fresh start. I loved the house, and chose it because it was situated on a cute little close. It made me feel safe, being surrounded by neighbours. I've always lived behind big electric gates in the middle of nowhere, with no one around – where nobody could hear my screams.

\*\*\*\*\*

George was visiting a lot and the space between us had meant he was on his best behaviour, but I was reluctant to let him come back full time, so he was still mainly staying with his parents.

One thing I did know was just how bad his drug addiction had become. It was one of the reasons I wasn't keen on having him back full time, even though we were sleeping together again by this point. Even as I write that sentence it makes me feel like a weak person. The thought of sleeping with him now turns my stomach, but back then I seemed to be powerless. I was pathetic. It seems to be a pattern when it comes to men.

# The Kids Aren't Alright

George was staying regularly and I would just keep an eye on him, knowing his mental state wasn't good, but again, hoping maybe if we got back together he would change. But he made it so difficult. It was like he deliberately took the hardest path possible, rather than get the help he needed. He was so, so troubled.

He always had a foot in the dark side and he used to practice black magic, as he was obsessed with the occult.

I remember when we were living in Chinnor, George was messing with dark forces. I used to find these dead flies in the bathroom all the time. Hundreds of them, scattered all over the floor. We'd hoover them up and then a couple of days later, they'd be back. Now that alone is enough to freak anyone out, but I later found out George was practising black magic in that same bathroom. I have no idea what it entailed and I don't want to know, all I know is it brought with it inevitable bad luck.

Strange things started happening in the house. Creepy, unexplained things that scared me so much we had an actual paranormal investigative team come out.

Max was still being really naughty. One day I caught him trying to tie curtains around his neck which really freaked me out – how would he know to do that at that age?

Another time I thought I saw Lilly walking through her bedroom – only Lilly was at a sleepover that night.

And then, one day George woke up and half of his face was paralysed. We later found out he had Bell's Palsy, a temporary condition which causes weakness to one side of the face, making it look as if you've had a stroke. I tell you what, I must have Bell's Palsy all over my body the amount of fucking times I kept sleeping with him, I was that weak.

There was too much darkness surrounding us. I was starting to think a spirit was in the house, possessing us.

So when these paranormal people came in they brought a spirit box with them, which is a piece of equipment that allows ghosts to communicate with you.

Turns out there was a ghost called John haunting the place. John told us that he was the one who'd done that to George's face and he was after my son. He wanted Max out of the house and that was why the boy had been playing with the curtains that time. Suffice to say, I was freaked out.

We saw pictures of the demon's face, weird shapes and flashes. We saw a huge orb above DJ's head. We even heard John's voice – and it scared the shit out of me.

A medium came in and blessed the house, she demanded John leave and, to my huge relief, it appears he did.

Despite the exorcism, life in the house continued to be unhappy. So while I was satisfied that they'd banished John, the doubt remained. Maybe the little bastard was still lurking about, because things kept going wrong even after I was assured he was back in the afterlife, where he belonged.

I think, though the whole 'John' experience scared the shit out of me, George loved it and felt a strong connection with the dead as a result. In fact I later found out he was doing more and more black magic and he'd refer to me as his Devil Angel while practising spells in the bathroom. I'm absolutely convinced his Bell's Palsy was a result of him messing with the occult – and not just because John took the credit for it. I really believe George had one foot on earth and one foot in the dark side.

By October 2015, George was basically living with us again in Crowborough and the beatings were back to being a regular occurrence. He'd started keeping these weird weapons in the house, including a taser gun. One day I caught Molly playing with it, thinking it was a torch, which was enough to freak me out, had I not also seen the 14-inch hunting knife stored next to it in the wardrobe.

After seeing my mum get stabbed when I was a kid, after being held at knife point when I lived with Mark, I was terrified of knives. Having this weapon in my house was horrifying to me. Especially knowing George the way I did. If he'd had a bout of psychosis there's no telling what he could do with that thing.

One night, when we hadn't been in Crowborough very long, George and I decided to go for a drink down the local pub in an effort to get to know the area.

Of course the night didn't go smoothly. He got drunk and ended up in a fight with these two young guys. I don't even recall how it started but I know it resulted in them running away after I told them, "You'd better step away, or he WILL kill you".

We headed home, George in an angry stupor, me just exasperated and fuming. We'd only just moved here and already it was kicking off. He was always after a fight. It clearly didn't matter who it was with!

We got home and he took out the hunting knife.

"Those lads are on their way here, Kerry, I know they are…" he said as he started to clutch at the huge weapon.

"They're not George, just leave it. Please, they're gone now," I begged, knowing his temper was now starting to take over and he wasn't thinking rationally.

"Shut up you c**t!" He yelled and punched me several times in the face. "They're coming to the house!"

He ripped a patch of my hair right out of my head, leaving

me with a huge bald spot. He dragged me through the house and jumped on me, kicking and punching relentlessly.

I was left crumpled in a heap on the floor, shaking uncontrollably. He spat on me and went upstairs to the bedroom, no doubt watching out the window, expecting these lads to show up. Of course, they never did.

I slept on the sofa that night, in pain, shaken, but grateful he hadn't used the knife.

I woke up the next morning and that was where Lilly found me, and when she applied the make-up to my bruises, in sad silence.

People may wonder why I didn't call the police at that point. But I had my reasons. We'd only just moved and I couldn't bear that sort of attention on me. I didn't want the neighbours to judge me like that, not when we'd only just moved in. And I couldn't face the wrath of the media once they inevitably got wind of the story. I didn't want the drama.

I was supposed to be on Big Brother's Bit On The Side a couple of days later.

"You can't go on TV looking like that," George told me once the bruises had come out, big, black, shiny.

"It's fine, I'll cover it with make-up" I protested, desperately not wanting to give up the job.

"No you bloody won't."

He rang my manager Paul.

"Kerry's not doing the show," he told him. "She got pissed up and fell down the stairs and she has two black eyes as a result."

I couldn't believe what I was hearing. The lies were spilling out of his mouth, like it was the most natural thing in the world. It was terrifying. At least Paul knew straight away those bruises weren't my doing. He knew exactly what George was like. But it begged the question, what the hell was next in store? He throws me down the stairs in a moment of madness and everyone thinks it's self-inflicted? He could quite literally kill me and get away with it.

It was at that moment I decided to take pictures of my injuries. I sent them to my mum and Paul and told them: "If anything happens to me – it's not my doing. It'll be George's fault and you need to know that."

Mum deleted the pics soon after from her phone and so did I. There's no way in hell I could risk George finding them.

*****

Breaking point came one night when we were chilling with the kids, including one of Heidi's school friends. It was our Friday family movie night, a much loved tradition in our house. We were getting ready to watch Pitch Perfect 2.

Before the film started, George told me he was popping out to get some cigarettes from the garage, which is less than five minutes up the road.

He was gone for nearly an hour.

When he came home he'd brought two bottles of Prosecco, which I had no intention of drinking. It made me suspicious right away. There was an ulterior motive here. A woman's instinct is a powerful thing. Why was he bringing me alcohol, which I hadn't asked for? Why had he been gone for an hour? Something wasn't adding up.

"Oh shit, I've forgotten the cigs, I'll have to go back." he said. It was the whole reason he went to the shop in the first place. So to be gone for an hour, come back with no cigarettes, I just knew something was up. My instinct told me he'd gone to call whoever the hell it was he was getting his gear from. But I doubted myself because there was no way he knew anyone in the area who dealt drugs. We'd only just moved here, I thought. Honestly, I don't know how he found it – he was like a bloody hound dog.

But as soon as he came back in the house for the second time, I only had to look at him and I could tell. He somehow became sheepish, childlike when he was on cocaine and it didn't take a genius to work out he was off his head.

He went straight into the garden. I followed him.

"Where the bloody hell have you been?" I was raging. "You've been on the coke haven't you?"

He denied it to my face.

"You have. I can tell. Don't you dare do drugs when my kids are here. What are you playing at? It's Friday night movie night, not only have we got all five kids here, we've got Heidi's friend too! Why are you ruining it?! Get the hell out of my house!"

But of course, George being George didn't go anywhere. Instead he went straight upstairs to my bedroom.

I could see Molly was on edge, despite the fact the kids hadn't heard a word of this exchange, so I went and sat with her, just to give her some unspoken reassurance.

That night I slept on the sofa. I couldn't bear to be around George.

The next morning I went upstairs to see if he was asleep – or, even better, gone. But instead I found him sat in the corner of the bedroom, in a wicker chair, clutching a bag of white powder, hoovering up more drugs. It was 8am.

# The Kids Aren't Alright

I couldn't believe it but I knew I had to sort the situation before the kids found out. He was high as a kite, so I brought him a bottle of beer to bring him back down. I put the rugby on the telly. Anything to pacify him.

I had to get the kids out of there. I loaded them into our people carrier and shuffled them out of the house. I ended up staying out for nine hours, sitting in a children's playground.

I remember putting the kids on this toy train and just watching it go round and round, hypnotically spinning, just like my brain was.

I was panicking the whole time about how the situation would resolve itself. Even as I write this I'm remembering the fear I felt and my stomach is in knots. I have such anxiety. Even now.

Finally we returned to the house. I was doing everything in my power to act normal in front of the kids, but my whole body was shaking. I just knew something big was about to happen. It was one of my many premonitions. When I feel like something's about to kick off, it usually does.

George was wandering around the kitchen, his eyes vacant. His face was completely expressionless. He looked at me and it was as if he didn't know who I was. It was like he wasn't there. The next thing I know he takes out his phone. He was examining the blank screen, peering at it, genuinely believing monsters were inside his mobile, coming for him.

I had to handle him with kid gloves. I was trying to be gentle, knowing he was in full psychosis. I had six kids in the house and now my huge, 6ft 4in husband was acting like this. My adrenaline took over and I gently took him upstairs. I went to make him some dinner.

I reached up to the cupboard with shaking hands to start preparing his meal, when the phone rang.

It was East Sussex police.

"We've received a missed call from this number," said a kindly voice on the other end of the line.

Oh God.

"Erm, it wasn't me," I replied, genuinely confused as I hadn't called the police and had no intention of doing so, for all the reasons I mentioned earlier. I didn't need that sort of drama and reputation following me around, not in my new home. "I've been out all day, you must have the wrong place."

I hung up.

A few minutes later the phone rang again.

"We are getting calls from this number relating to a domestic disturbance," again, that voice.

"It must be my little girl, messing about," I said, my voice starting to crack. "It definitely wasn't me."

But by now I'd figured it out. Don't ask me how, but I just knew it was George.

And right on cue, that's when I heard his voice. He'd picked up the upstairs phone and was now on the line with me and the police.

"It wasn't the kids," he said, completely calmly. "It was me. My wife's trying to murder me. She's going to kill me."

My stomach dropped. My first thought wasn't for me, it was for those six kids. The eerie calmness in his voice signalled something terrifying was about to happen. I had to get them out. I tried to stay calm.

I hung up. George was still rambling down the phone. I took my mobile, called our neighbour Amelia, the first friend

I'd made at the new address and who happened to be a police officer, and asked her to take the kids.

She came over and realised the enormity of the situation. She immediately took the children over to hers. I'd hid myself in the utility room, sobbing, shaking. I was shitting myself. I was genuinely scared for my life. I called Amelia again on my mobile from my hiding place to check the children were safe, and she came straight back over, sneaking around the back of the house, returning to protect me. She was so calm and so brave, while I was sat there, crouched in the corner of the room, shaking violently.

And then I heard the sirens.

Thanks to his record, the police had a big red mark against George's name and so any disturbance or threat would be taken seriously from our household.

Scores and scores of officers arrived at the house, much to my relief. Four cars and a van in the tiny cul de sac I'd only been living in for three months. But I didn't care anymore, I was too frightened. By this point I just needed George to be gone.

An officer managed to coax him out of the house. He was calm, measured but kept saying monsters were after him. It was a truly tragic scene.

The second I knew he was out I ran upstairs to Molly's room. She and Lilly shared the top floor, so I went to hide there while the police gathered George's stuff.

I don't think anyone will understand just how frightened I was in those moments. I can't even put into words how terrifying it was. It was like everything I'd been through up until that point had been building to it.

The police came up to the bedroom.

"George wants to get some of his stuff," an officer told me.

"Well he can't come near me," I pleaded. "You'll have to get his stuff yourself. But just so you know there's a huge hunting knife and a taser gun in the wardrobe."

I was crying hysterically at this point – the policeman couldn't hide his shock.

"My daughter was playing with it, it's disguised as a torch."

George was put in the back of a van. I went downstairs to the kitchen. I was only able to leave the bedroom once I was certain he was gone.

A policeman sat me down and gently asked me if anything else had happened… and just like that, it all came spewing out of me. Encouraged by George's mum, who was listening on speaker phone at this point and begging me to come clean, I let it all out. It was like I had no control over the words I was saying. All this built-up fear and anxiety, all the secrets, they all came pouring out. It was the first time anyone had really asked me what was going on and suddenly I couldn't shut up. I told the police everything. I told them about the beatings, the threats, the drugs, the spitting – I must have spoken for hours, unburdening myself of these awful, dreadful secrets that had been weighing me down for years.

The police put an order on George that ensured he didn't come near me at that point. As far as I know he went back to his parents. Despite the fact they were clearly as scared of him as I was, he had nowhere else to go.

The police were fantastic. They put lights up at the front and back of the house, I was given a domestic abuse support worker called Tracey to talk to and a panic alarm – which George would later refer to as the rape alarm – and which they told me I had to wear. I had a code word for when I felt like I was in danger. During one of our many comforting talks, it took me aback when Tracey looked at me, with pity in her eyes and told me, "You know, this isn't normal. You don't have to put up with this."

I burst into tears.

She gave me facts and statistics about abusive relationships and I really believe it was her guidance that gave me the strength to get the ball rolling and start getting myself out of the marriage for good. My mum and Danielle were my rocks back then too, Mum came and stayed with me and sat in meetings with me and Tracey. But it wasn't a quick fix, these women spent a long time trying to build me back up from that whole hideous experience – I was so, so damaged by this point.

George was later charged with assault by beating and possessing a banned weapon and had to appear in court to answer bail.

It was at that point I wanted him out of my life for good. I was done.

But of course, a tale as old as time, the abused woman never fully escapes.

We managed to stay split up for a good few weeks while he was out on bail, but by January 2016, he had wormed his way back in.

We'd began to meet in secret. He made me feel like he was sorry and as a result I was almost powerless.

I remember one time the police came to check up on me, little knowing George was inside the house. We were in there with my aunt Angela. It was night-time and George and I were in my bedroom, while Angela was outside the door. She saw the police car through the window and immediately came to tell us.

"The police are here," she whispered.

But rather than be grateful for the heads up, George came up behind her, put his hand over her mouth and muttered through gritted teeth, "Don't say a fucking word."

We were all frozen. If he was caught he would've been arrested on the spot for breaking the conditions of his bail. Mind you, he always felt he was above the law. He was dead cocky when it came to bail. He'd take the piss, asking the judge why he couldn't get his hair cut and stupid things like that. He thought he was dead funny and I'd fake laugh along with him to keep him happy.

Meanwhile, Molly was downstairs and upon hearing the police at the door, she instinctively turned the TV off and slid down the back of the sofa to hide. My kids shouldn't be thinking like that, it shouldn't be their first instinct to react that way, but there we were. Always controlled by fear.

George was so manipulative – I'd end up apologising to him, begging him to return to me, even after all the help I'd been given by Tracey and the police.

It was so fucked up.

I eventually dropped the charges and we reconciled.

If you're angry reading this, angry that I went back to him yet again, believe me, I am too.

But I just can't explain the thought process. I missed him. The kids missed him. It was like I couldn't function without him. Because he was so controlling, I'd become completely co-dependent.

And believe it or not, I felt safer having him at home. At least I knew where he was and what mood he was in. When he wasn't around, I would be forever on edge wondering what he could be planning. Would he be out trying to take the kids? Stalking the school? It was easier to have him under the same roof.

Plus I kept using his mental illness as an excuse for his behaviour. I'll admit it, I was weak. I didn't want another failed marriage. I didn't want another baby daddy not living in the same house as his child.

Of course the papers had a field day and couldn't wait to spill the beans on my latest car crash of a marriage, so I was determined to make it work this time. We'd get George proper help. We'd get him off drugs and into some sort of treatment programme. The naysayers won't win. I WON'T fail. George WILL get better. But it never happened.

In fact after the charges were dropped, George obviously felt he was invincible and could get away with whatever he wanted. His nastiness, his spitefulness, the fact he was a narcissistic bully, was becoming unbearable. But I couldn't leave. I was living in a permanent state of fear.

I was fighting a losing battle. I was torn between not wanting another divorce and not wanting DJ to come from a broken family and keeping us safe. And, clichéd as it may be, I still loved the man.

It was an endless, vicious cycle of breaking up, making up, violence and sadness. Of course there were good times in between it all – there had to be to justify the fact I kept going back to him – but they were getting fewer and fewer.

Spilling my guts to the police signified the point of no return for us – but yet it didn't stop us. The reality was, I was stuck in something I was powerless to get out of.

I was failing as a mother and as a woman and I hated myself for it.

# 6

## Cutting Ties

Things came to a head in 2017.

George and I weren't getting on and we were fighting constantly. It was bad. Really bad. Of course it had been pretty awful in the years leading up to this point, but throughout it all I still loved him and I still believed I deserved the violence I was subjected to. I'd always known what I was getting into, after all.

But there came a point where it just wasn't sustainable anymore. The kids were starting to suffer. And it was becoming more and more apparent just how unstable George was. Every day he was in the house I was risking my life. I was risking my children's lives. And I couldn't keep doing it. He was becoming ugly to me. The more I saw of his personality, the less attractive he was. I was still sexually attracted to him, don't get me wrong. And that was my biggest weakness. But as a human being, he was becoming detestable.

I was given an amazing opportunity to join reality show Big Brother again towards the end of 2016, to take part in their Celebrity version, for a task as a returning contestant. The pay wasn't brilliant, but a job is a job and money's money and I thought getting back on TV could really help me get more work, especially after the bad press I'd had since mine and George's last break-up.

I was really excited and George even agreed to it, but as the time got closer, it soon became *very* clear that he was getting cold feet. He wasn't going to allow me to do it.

Whether or not he was worried about not being there to control me in the CBB house or he just hated the thought of me doing something independently of him, he was having none of it.

"You'll go on that show over my dead body" he told me as we spoke about it with Molly the night before I was due to go.

"But George, we desperately need the money," I pleaded. "You don't have a job and we need the cash. And this could be a great opportunity for us. I won't even be gone long. It's only for three days – you can stay with the kids and watch me on the show every night!"

The problem was, I had already signed the contract to go into the BB house. I remember getting the call and being so scared to tell George, he always wanted to be by my side so you can imagine my dread at having to tell him I was going away for three days. But the money would pay the council tax, the gas and electricity – and even a bit of the rent.

The chauffeur was all booked to pick me up. George wasn't going to let me go without a fight.

"I take it you're gonna pay me to look after the kids while you're gone," he said, as if such a request was the most normal thing a parent could ask their partner.

I was gobsmacked. I could barely answer before he looked

me square in the eye, and in the most sinister voice I'd ever heard, said: "Leave those kids with me and watch what fucking happens." I went into the spare bedroom, sat down on the bed and started crying. I couldn't believe this was happening to me. I have always been so professional when it comes to my work. How the hell was I going to get out of this job? I was so embarrassed.

I remember he was wearing just a t-shirt and y-fronts and he followed me into the room, where he started slagging me off.

"You think you'll be going on national television, on your holidays, getting pissed up with a load of celebrities?" he goaded me.

"We need the bloody money George!," I shouted back through sobs. "Why the hell don't you get a job, eh? You too good to get a proper job, George?"

I was so fed up that I felt brave enough to say it to his face, but his reaction scared me.

"Yeah," he snarled, as he lent right into me. "I am too good to get a job."

In that moment all I saw was pure ugliness. I always, always fancied George, regardless of the things he put me through, but at this point in our relationship, he was just a nasty, ugly waste of space to me. He reiterated his statement about leaving him with the children – that I should beware what happens, and so the conversation ended there.

I called my manager straight away and told him I wasn't doing the show. I wasn't going to risk my kids for anything. And there was no way I couldn't take George's threats seriously. By this point he was so violent and so abusive, I believe wholeheartedly he would've killed them if I'd taken the job.

# Cutting Ties

I came off the phone and saw Molly looking right at me. It was a look of total and utter disappointment. It was a look that said: 'You're weak, Mum. You're weak and pathetic.'

I swear my heart broke into a million pieces in that moment. And it had nothing to do with losing a promising TV deal. Seeing my first-born baby girl so badly let down by me, witnessing a man completely and utterly control her mummy, was one of the lowest points of my life.

That was it. I never, ever wanted any of my children to look at me in that way, ever again.

I know deep down that seeing me like that was what prompted Molly to move to Ireland that year. She was desperate to go to college and live a normal life and she opted to do that in Dublin, where she could live with her grandparents, Brian's mum and dad.

I was devastated but I put on a front, not wanting her to feel as trapped as I did in Crowborough.

She never explicitly said it, but I'm absolutely certain she just wanted to get away from the fear and the pain George brought to our lives. And how could I ever truly forgive myself for allowing him in like I did? I felt that I was responsible for her sadness. I allowed this to happen.

But either way I felt like I was losing Molly. And suddenly, my marriage just wasn't worth it. I had fought as hard as I could. Her look of utter disdain was the last straw for me.

In my head, the wheels were now in motion. I was getting out... for good.

*****

What followed was another real lightbulb moment for me. It came at the funeral of Danielle's dad, Martin, who'd passed away in the March.

It was a conflicting time for Danielle, who had recently reunited with her sister, Mel, after ten years apart. She knew only too well what I'd been going through, as Mel had been out in LA living a hell of her own with an abusive husband. It had scared Danielle witless and caused her so many sleepless nights.

The poor cow had my problems to deal with as well and to this day I'll never forget her support, especially when she had so much going on in her own life at the time.

Anyway, Mel had found the strength to get out of the relationship and had managed to get back to her family in England to reconnect with Martin and Danielle just days before he died.

It had meant so much to the whole family and I think in the back of my mind I was always envious of Mel for managing to escape. I was so pleased she did, for both her and Danielle's sake. Danielle was so, so happy to know her sister was safe. Alive.

I started to think that maybe my kids, especially Molly, would be just as happy if I was strong enough to finally leave George.

We all gathered at the funeral one chilly day up in Leeds, where Martin was laid to rest at St Aidan's Church.

Danielle had her new fella with her but I could see she was emotional. I squeezed her hand.

"I love you and I'm here for you"

She looked back at me with wet eyes. "You too babe."

Now *that's* real love.

It was a beautiful service that opened to the sounds of Bob

Marley singing Three Little Birds. His unmistakable voice rang out across the church.

*Don't worry about a thing / Cause every little thing, gonna be alright.*

I looked around and I had the most bizarre feeling. Seeing all these people, dressed in back, fighting back tears as this wonderful, uplifting song played – would this be my fate too? Will it be my funeral next?

The thought was chilling and felt like a dark premonition. I shivered and struggled to shake it off.

At the end of the ceremony I saw a friend of ours, Glen, gifting his friend's kids some money. It was a really lovely gesture and showed how generous this man was. But all I kept thinking was, 'George wouldn't be able to do something like this for our friends' kids. Because he doesn't have any money of his own. He always uses my card. He doesn't have a job.'

The thought wouldn't leave my mind – all I could see when I looked at George now was ugliness. A con artist who never wanted to pay his way, he was never legit.

I felt like a switch had gone off in my head. I turned my back on him and went up to Danielle.

"I don't love George anymore," I told her.

She put her arm around me and we walked together in silence.

It took a few more weeks to finally leave George. I was scared – no, terrified – about being alone again but I couldn't shake the premonition I had at the funeral. I was so sure if I didn't get out of the marriage, I would be the next in a coffin.

We had many big rows in those final days. He would constantly tell me, "You're mine until I die, Kerry. Mine!"

But I knew I had to find the strength to finish it.

In the end, George left the house in Crowborough with surprisingly minimal fuss one perfectly ordinary day in June 2017. After everything we'd been through I was expecting him to trash the place, or make some last desperate threats or even ramp up the charm in an attempt to turn things around.

But the reality was, he was probably as done with me as I was with him. The sadness and pain we inflicted upon each other was too much. It was the biggest relief to me when he left, despite the fact I was heartbroken that another marriage had failed and even though, deep down, I still longed for the old George to come back, the one who would have me in fits of giggles.

It's like any break-up. You could truly hate the person and still feel so, so sad it didn't work out.

Once George was gone, I sat Molly and Lilly down and I profusely apologised to them. I knew I'd done to them exactly what my mum had done to me, and that's something I never, ever thought I'd do.

I was ashamed, sad and exhausted.

"Women need to be strong," I explained. "And no matter what, there's no excuse for any woman to be treated like this. I don't want you to think for a second there is. No one deserves this and I'm so, so sorry you witnessed it."

I remember crying.

"I've always been a strong mum," I wept. "But now you've seen I'm not that strong after all, and I'm so devastated I can't take that back."

With little DJ still so young, we wanted to make things as easy as possible for her when it came to the transition of having two parents living apart. Despite George's threats to the kids, I wanted to make sure he still had access to her. I was seriously thinking about supervised visits only, but when I saw the two of them together, I just couldn't fathom him hurting her. Maybe that was naive of me, but he was still her dad and I wanted to do everything I could to keep her life as unaffected as possible.

And of course I wanted to shield Max and Heidi from the pain as well. After all they called George "daddy" too.

Sadly George showed his true, cruel colours when it came to those two. After we split he chose to completely discard them, refusing to acknowledge their existence and claiming he wanted nothing to do with them, only DJ.

My heart absolutely broke for those kids. They didn't understand why, after everything, George was suddenly gone and only wanted to see DJ. Yes, they understood DJ was his biological daughter, but children don't think in those terms when they have a bond with someone. To them they were being chucked to the side, like rubbish in a bin bag.

Of all the things George put us through, that's one thing I struggle to get my head around now. How could he possibly do that to those little children who idolised him? He'd been in their lives since they were tiny, and now he was making it very clear he didn't want them – all to punish me.

I hated him for doing that. And I wonder even now the effect it's had on them, especially Max, who's watched two father figures just turn their backs on him. For Heidi, I fear she'll always have trust issues with men as a result. She was truly troubled when George did that to her. But I suppose I knew in my heart she'd be better off in the long run without him, so I gritted my teeth, allowed George to be petty and break her heart, in the hope that she'd soon forget him.

*****

He was high as a kite the day he crawled naked, screaming, onto a rooftop in Liverpool.

I was down south with the kids. It was a few weeks after the split and the space between us seemed to make things more amicable.

He was still being a dickhead to the four older kids, but DJ was seeing him fairly regularly and he was calmer, somehow. I had felt at peace with my decision to leave the marriage, though George was turning on the charm whenever we were together and it took every fibre of my being not to jump into bed with him.

It's the weirdest thing. I had convinced myself I didn't love him anymore. I didn't even particularly like him, but I still had this primal urge to sleep with him and that's something that didn't seem to go away. At one point in those few weeks I even wondered if we'd somehow work through our issues and get back together. Was there hope for us?

But then he ended up on that bloody roof and I guess in many ways, that really was the final nail in the coffin.

I was washing up when it happened.

I got a call from my manager, Paul. "Kerry, I've had the papers on the phone, George was seen crawling around naked on a roof," he told me, with more than a hint of exasperation in his voice.

I wasn't quite sure what I was hearing.

"What are you on about?" I asked him, confused. "I haven't seen or heard from George for three days. I've been trying to call him so he can speak to DJ but he hasn't answered his phone all weekend. What's going on?"

Apparently the papers had a video of my estranged husband, screaming on the roof of a house, totally naked.

Paul then sent me the footage.

What I saw almost knocked me for six. It was one of the most disturbing things I'd ever laid my eyes on – and yet what I was seeing was all too familiar.

'Kill me!' He kept yelling as the grainy camera footage panned in on him. Actually it was more like barking. Despite his massive frame he sounded like a wounded animal. He was cupping his private parts and lying on the roof, his head raised slightly as police begged him to come down. He was frothing at the mouth. There were people in the windows watching. Whichever scumbag filmed it could be heard laughing from behind the camera.

It was George in full psychosis mode. He wasn't violent, he wasn't spitting or angry and he didn't have a fire in his eyes. He was just totally lost. Even through the tiny mobile phone screen, I could see in his face he was frightened, and the short sharp yells coming from his mouth were just as frightening to hear. He was completely drugged up and it was clear from the video he was in a bad way.

I was shaking like a leaf watching the footage. I think it was the first time I truly knew in my heart it was over, forever. This wasn't even about me and George and our relationship anymore. This was about a man who was so, so troubled he needed immediate help. And I could no longer be relied on to give him that help. It was too much. My heart sank as a mixture of pity, sadness and sheer terror came over me. George couldn't come back from this. A pathetic, crying, frightened man-beast, naked on a roof, frothing at the mouth, high on cocaine? There had to be a line (pardon the pun). I couldn't put myself or my kids through it anymore. I could take the beatings. I could almost understand the anger. But to see him this way – it was like the hope finally left my heart.

Because of my experience of drugs in the past, and knowing how I got myself clean, I was so sure I could do the same for George. It was now clear as day, it wasn't meant to be.

Don't get me wrong, I'd seen George like this before in the privacy of our home. He would get psychosis and hallucinate and I would gently try and pacify him until it passed.

But he was a big guy and when he got like that you couldn't control him, as we know from the Friday movie night debacle.

He used to say monsters were after him. He told me he'd killed people. Of course I don't think that's true, but I think he had these fantasies of being in the mafia. That's the only way I can explain it. He'd see Tony Soprano on the telly and think that was him. He had so many mental issues, he was so tortured.

But I'd never seen him like this in such a public setting. People were laughing at him. The police were there. It was the saddest, most pathetic sight and it somehow felt worse because it was all so… exposed.

I managed to keep the video out of the press on the grounds of mental health and I don't have any intentions of it seeing the light of day now, mainly out of respect for DJ. I don't want her to ever watch it.

And I won't include any stills from the video in this book

either, as I don't see the point of posting pictures of a now dead man, naked on a roof, begging for help. The papers made a huge deal about it at the time and that was bad enough even without the footage doing the rounds.

The first time I saw it I was horrified and it made me question yet again why he was so insistent on doing drugs. I never really understood it and I didn't throughout our entire marriage.

If he wanted to take drugs that much, why didn't he do it with his mates on a Saturday night? Why take a shed load of coke and come back to the house where I'm watching telly with the five kids?

And why do it at all knowing how badly it seemed to affect him? What pleasure was he getting out of it? It never made sense to me. I know people still do coke – and that's their choice, I'm not here to judge anyone, even though I wouldn't touch it ever again, but you could see, when he was on that roof, it was too much for George.

To my knowledge he came down without too much of a fight in the end. Maybe he sobered up, maybe the specialist police officers there figured out how to calm his mind, or maybe he just came to his senses all on his own. Either way he called me shortly after and told me he'd tried to kill himself.

Now I know for a fact he would never, ever try and kill himself. For all his genuine mental health issues, he was just too much of a narcissist to do that. I knew he was covering up the fact he was on drugs.

At the time I truly believed seeing George like that was the end of the line for me and sure enough, things went from amicable to pretty hideous soon after. I was done. Emotionally drained and devastated and feeling sick with worry that the next 'roof' incident could be his last. I didn't have the mental capacity to deal with it anymore.

And seeing that was the case, George turned nasty again. He began publicly accusing me of violence and did everything he could to slander my name.

He even gave an interview to a national newspaper in which he lied through his teeth and said I was the abusive one in the marriage. That I was responsible for all his troubles.

"She flips her lid about anything," he said. "She'll scream and shout, then she gets very aggressive. I've had to report her to the police in the past. People think of her as this bubbly, lovable lass. But the reality is very different."

Let me tell you now, the reality certainly *was* different. Different to whatever hideous fantasy George had conjured up in his head.

I was so sick of it. It was the lies that scared me more than anything. How he was able to deceive people, right to their faces without a hint of remorse. I couldn't get my head around it.

And I felt enormous sadness that things had reached this point. How had we got to this place?

I still looked back at the early days, how I felt around him and how he'd made me feel protected and lucky to be with him. Even writing it down, thinking about it, makes me smile, remembering those times. Oh such conflicted feelings!

I yearned for those days, but the man George had become was a different beast entirely and I knew we'd never get back there.

But I was so sure he'd try and win me back again, try and manipulate his way back into my bed at least. I had to take drastic measures to ensure that didn't happen.

So that's exactly what I did.

# 7

## The Rebound

As you can probably tell by now, breaking up with George was hugely traumatic and not the straightforward split I'd have hoped for, not least because we had a daughter together. His mental health was at an all time low and despite all his efforts to destroy my name with his lies (he was the biggest narcissist in the world, to the point I think he actually believed them), he'd still be trying to lure me back into bed whenever he was around. And I knew I was weak enough to fall for it. I was so damaged from what I'd been through. I needed to take action.

So, in what I can now see was a way-too-soon moment of madness, I dipped my toe in the dating pool again.

It was September 2017 and barely weeks since George and I had split, but I was ready to prove a point at least. The 'relationship' (if you could call it that) which followed was a strange one. It won't go down in the history books as a great romance, that's for sure! And because I've been burned way too often by exes looking to make a quick buck out of me, I won't name him in this book. I don't want to give him the satisfaction or risk him trying to sell stories on me again. Not that he'd have much to go on. I can tell you everything right here.

Let's call him 'Mike'.

Mike was a prime example of getting under someone to get over someone, but it was certainly significant for one big reason.

I was still reeling from the whole George debacle, which, as you can imagine, was still occupying most of my thoughts. The way everything had played out, from those last rows to that awful situation on the roof, my head was still all over the place. I guess I wasn't in the right frame of mind to date anyone, and isn't it always the way in those situations where you end up making the biggest mistakes of your life?

As I struggled to come to terms with the trauma that had been the last few years of my life, I found myself in the company of this alright looking guy, a bit of a wannabe actor, who seemed like a charmer, but, as is often the case with my love interests, turned out to be anything but.

I was immediately taken with Mike. Of course, as is my luck, reports soon surfaced suggesting his past behaviour wasn't whiter than white. But for me he was just a perfect distraction from the heartbreak and I wasn't looking for anything serious, so the obvious red flags didn't faze me.

Just to have someone flirt with me lifted my confidence at a time when, in reality, my heart was shattered into a million pieces.

Even though in my mind George and I were done for good and I'd finally been strong enough to leave, it brought me little comfort. This was still yet another failed marriage and the whole scenario had left me incredibly depressed. I never wanted my daughter to be without a full time dad! I did everything to save that relationship and now, finding myself single again, it was a low point in my life. Although I knew, deep down, a divorce was the right thing to do.

Someone like Mike was a rare case for me. I've never slept around. Hand on my heart I can hold my head up high and say that. No judgement to anyone who does, it's just not me. Of course the press would've had you believe differently, five kids by three men and all that, but the truth is I fell in love with three men and married them. Yes, I had an affair behind Mark's back, which was the best thing I ever did because it gave me the courage to leave him, but I don't have too many notches on my bedpost, that's for sure.

For a serial bride like me, I was happy enough to be dating again. Mike was fun – and he provided an escape of sorts. The reason being is that I knew if I slept with someone else the door would be closed on me and George forever. Yes, there was a divorce on the table. Yes, in my head, after everything, there was no chance of a reconciliation.

But that tiny voice in the back of my head knew George's ways. He'd be able to win me back just by clicking his fingers if he wanted to. I had to do everything in my power to make sure that didn't happen.

My plan? Well, I knew he'd never come back if he thought I was 'soiled' goods. If I slept with Mike, it was my way out for good. It was what I genuinely wanted. To be honest, it was what I *needed*.

So Mike was my big rebound – and, as it turned out, my next big mistake.

\*\*\*\*\*

I got pregnant. It must have been within two weeks of meeting him. I remember finding out just before I went on stage with Atomic Kitten at a gig in Scotland.

Something wasn't quite right and I was well versed enough in pregnancy to know the signs. I took a test and waited for the result to come through on that tiny godforsaken stick.

Two lines.

Rather than experiencing the sheer joy I felt when I discovered I was having my other babies, I dropped to the floor in disbelief, hands shaking, heart pounding. No, no no no no. How the bloody hell had this happened? I was careful, I was on the pill – and I even took several morning-after pills. I felt so bewildered and suddenly quite desperate. My mind was racing as I imagined having a child with a man I didn't know at all. A life trapped, the poor baby a product of separate parents, judgement from people who didn't know me… the hell I would face from George.

This wasn't supposed to happen. After the trauma of the last few years, Mike was supposed to be easy and fun, a way of moving on and closing the door on my marriage for good. This relationship wasn't supposed to go down this road. Certainly not yet.

In my panicked haze I immediately booked an appointment for an abortion. Tash Hamilton, a huge support at the time, was going to go with me.

But I couldn't go through with it. I couldn't even make the journey to go there, I was too overwhelmed with the guilt and the trauma of it all.

"Pull yourself together, Kerry," I sternly told myself as I grappled with the confusion and panic.

I booked another appointment.

No, not gonna happen.

I tried another. Third time lucky. But yet again, I couldn't bring myself to walk through the clinic doors. I talked myself out of aborting my baby on every occasion.

I adore kids and even though I was not in love with Mike, it just didn't feel right to terminate the child. It went against everything I thought I believed in.

I remember crying myself to sleep most nights during that time, debating what to do and how to manage. The fear, the panic, those early pregnancy hormones making me feel horrific too.

I remember my mum held me in her arms, like I was a baby again. I was bawling my eyes out.

"I can't go through with it, Mum, I can't!"

Was I referring to the pregnancy? Or the abortion? I don't think I knew myself, but either way I was totally trapped.

All I wanted was for someone to push me down the stairs so I'd have an accident and the baby would go away.

It's the most horrible thing to say, and even writing this down it brings tears to my eyes, but the truth is, deep down, I didn't want that baby inside of me. I wasn't connected to the pregnancy at all. I didn't want another child with another man. And it's not like I wasn't careful. I was on the pill! I wasn't being reckless, this wasn't something I deserved, this was a complete accident. A very unhappy one.

It took a lot of soul searching, crying and talking with Mike, a man I barely knew. But eventually, the maternal side of me won out and we reluctantly agreed to keep the baby. We had very early pre-natal blood tests to reveal the gender and I don't remember feeling anything when we were told she was a little girl.

Life went on for a brief moment, mostly in a sad daze as I tried to convince myself I was doing the right thing.

But then fate stepped in.

On one of the cold, lonely nights that followed, I remember waking up – it must have been three o'clock in the morning – and feeling this strange pain. I shouted to Lilly to come in, immediately struck by the unusual sensation – and then I saw the blood in my bed.

I went to the toilet, and then this thing fell out of me. Right out of my womb. It was a huge clot. A mixture of fear and relief flooded through me. I knew I was losing the baby.

I was taken away in an ambulance, but, as tends to be the way with me, nothing from then on was straightforward. In fact, I was barely able to stay in the hospital for more than five minutes.

I was supposed to be going to India you see, where I was doing a gig with Michelle Heaton. My manager, Paul, told me that if I didn't get on that plane, I'd be sued by the concert promoter for £20k. Which as you can imagine, at that point in my life, scared the hell out of me.

I had an intravenous drip in my arm, from where I'd been checked in at hospital for scans, but I ripped it out of my skin and instead I legged it to the airport, the fresh blood still drying between my legs.

What the doctors must have thought of me!

I bled the whole plane journey to India. I think I blocked it all out at the time, I remember it feeling completely surreal, like I was in another body. As well as the usual discomfort of a long distance flight, travelling under those circumstances was beyond anything I'd experienced and I honestly think I was numb.

That said, I can't say I was devastated. Having never truly felt connected to this baby, it felt like fate to be losing her. Like it was meant to be. But at the same time, knowing the little girl was dying inside me while I was 30,000 feet up in the air on the way to a gig, was not pleasant in any way, shape or form. Seriously, my head was in a bad way.

I arrived safely in India and, being the professional I am, took to the stage to perform. And I remember feeling the blood running down the inside of my thighs as I belted out Atomic Kitten hits. Looking back now, I wonder what I must have been thinking and feeling in those moments. Because I sure as hell don't remember now. Surely it would've been absolutely horrific – and yet I carried on, singing and dancing and smiling for the crowd, who wouldn't have known anything was wrong. It feels like a surreal fever dream, looking back now.

After the gig, there was no hiding what was happening. I knew I had to get help. This wasn't something I could just walk away from, I had to see to it one way or another, as the bleeding wasn't letting up.

I was taken to hospital again, in this foreign country, where I was told the foetus was still in me and she still had a very, very faint heartbeat – but there was nothing the doctors could do. I stayed in hospital for a couple of days until eventually there was no heartbeat anymore. But the baby was still inside my belly.

The doctor said that the dead foetus could stay in the womb for up to three months before it would fall out naturally. Or I could have it removed before it got to that stage.

At least it was out of my hands. The baby's fate was determined by a higher power who I guess knew what was best for me. Essentially I was on the verge of miscarrying, as that child had not survived, but I suppose technically in the end I did have a termination, as she was removed from my body by a kind doctor.

Now remember, at this point I was a mum of five, my babies were – and still are – absolutely everything to me and it went against every single maternal instinct I had, but I knew this child was not meant to be.

Even now, I can't bring myself to refer to her as my daughter. It's not me being heartless, it's just my truth. A bleak, sad chapter in my life.

She hadn't been conceived in love, like my other children, I knew Mike and I were not meant to be together in the long term, but still – the mum in me! My heart ached for this little unborn baby but relief also drenched through me when she died. It was a strange, cruel situation that even now makes me feel guilty.

I was all alone in India at that point. Frightened, relieved, scared, in pain. I called up a close friend who hopped on a plane with her husband and came to see me at the hospital.

I've always managed to find myself making friends with people who turn out to be the lowest of the low, and this person, sadly, was no exception.

I was really fond of her and I actually thought she was one of the good ones, but what she did to take advantage of me upon arriving at the hospital is something I'll never, ever forget – or forgive.

Once there, when I was high on morphine, rather than console and comfort me, she filmed me, posted the video on Instagram and wrote the caption: 'This is Kerry Katona murdering her child'.

As soon as I'd found out what she'd done, my heart dropped. As you can imagine I became completely hysterical. Overcome with rage, heartache and betrayal – and I was all alone out there.

I had her take it down as soon as I could and, thank God, the press couldn't print it because it was medical information.

But my heart was broken. To this day I don't know why she did that to me. It still baffles me how anyone – especially a close friend – could be so cruel and evil and what on earth sort of satisfaction she could've possibly got from it.

Being in a foreign country, dealing with such an awful betrayal by a friend at such a traumatic moment and, of course, the abortion itself, left me drained.

But I know now what happened was a blessing. It sounds awful to say, but I never bonded with that foetus and I never think of her as my daughter. And I wonder if other women who have been through similar, unwanted pregnancies can relate. Should I feel guilty for not wanting my own child? Do I need to seek forgiveness for wishing her gone? Or can I hold my head high and say to this day that what transpired was right for me and my family?

Life isn't all sunshine and roses. It does throw these curveballs at you, because you know what? It's not a rom com. it's not bloody Love Actually. Life is hard and cruel and it presents these awful dilemmas. And this was one of them.

I ended things with Mike straight away. The way it all panned out with the baby, it truly was for the best.

I discovered pretty quickly he wasn't a great love, or a knight in shining armour.

Instead he seemed like a bit of a cad. He was just a fella who took me out for a few drinks – and who, momentarily, I was having a child with. It all finished as quickly as it started.

Of course he tried to sell stories on me after. Looking back I was big time tabloid fodder and I think he wanted to be famous. I think he loved the idea of being seen out and about with Kerry Katona. I'm glad I don't have any ties to him now.

I think I can only truly be open about this pregnancy now because George is dead.

It's not something I've ever been comfortable talking about publicly until now. I think part of that is because of how Mike would react – someone who I don't have in my life at all any more and I'm glad of it. But of course it was always on my mind, especially back when Mike and I decided to keep the baby, just how angry George would be by the situation.

I can see it now; the insults, the threats, I'm sure he would've tried to take DJ from me out of spite. Sleeping with another man was one way to ensure he'd never come back. But if he'd known I'd got myself pregnant so soon after splitting up with him, I think he actually would've returned to me. But only to kill me.

My close family and friends know, but to my knowledge George never got wind of it. If he did I'm certain I would've paid the price for it. Even though we were no longer together, he was still legally my husband and I can't imagine a scenario where he would've let me 'get away' with being impregnated by someone else.

It's hard to even fathom now, having another little girl running about, another potentially absent father and another school uniform to wash. I feel so removed from it.

## The Rebound

But that doesn't mean losing her hasn't affected me. Even now, it's one of the reasons I'm scared to have another child, although I know how much it would mean to Ryan.

After my hellish labour with DJ and then losing this baby, the idea of putting my body through it all again scares the hell out of me.

But we'll get to that.

# 8

## Time's Up

Of course I couldn't stay away from George. After everything I'd promised myself, throughout all the heartbreak, the pain, the pregnancy with Mike, I had completely and utterly convinced myself I would never go near him again.

We genuinely did break up that day in 2017 and I truly, truly believed it was over. And it was really, aside from the sex. The pull of the familiar meant we ended up sleeping together a couple more times – his charms worked as I feared they would, it never truly felt over – and even now the timeline of the various dalliances confuses me.

As I said, I naively thought being with Mike would mean he'd never touch me again, but George had a knack of surprising me.

He would woo me into bed and for a split second I might convince myself we belonged with one another. But then I'd soon come to my senses and remind him in no uncertain terms we were *not* back together.

Besides, I knew he had other women on the go too. He was using me, proving he still had that hold on me, ensuring I knew full well he could have me whenever he wanted me, regardless of the fact he was also sleeping with other girls.

So why did I keep going back? The same reason I always kept making bad choices. Self sabotage. To punish myself. Because I truly believed I deserved the heartache and the confusion.

It was a weird time, really. After the roof incident, knowing what bad shape his mental health was in, realising too the extent of his drug use, it should've been enough for me to stay away.

Back when we broke up, my feelings for him seemed to vanish overnight. It was as if a switch had gone off in my head and I was almost repulsed by him. But when he decided he wanted me back in his bed, I was basically powerless. All logic and good judgement went out of the window.

Of course looking back today I see things a little differently. He was a man with so many problems. He needed psychiatric help, rehab – hell, even jail could have done him some good, just so he could've taken time out to help himself. I can't blame him completely for his downfalls because he was so, so troubled. He was a narcissistic addict who just went too far and I was partly responsible for allowing him to get away with what he did for so long.

But this crazy situation couldn't go on forever. I couldn't keep going back to him, knowing I didn't really want him – something had to give.

Thank God it did.

George told the press he'd served me divorce papers in November 2017. The reality was quite different. What he actually 'served' me was a financial order. A list of all the things he wanted from me. He never once served me any divorce notification. He had no intention of divorcing me!

But I had every intention of making it happen.

I was so broke by this point I simply begged him for a quickie divorce online, £500, job done. I knew it was the only way to get out of our increasingly hopeless situation.

Of course he wasn't happy. He came around to my house. I remember he had a leather coat on, and he walked in, cool as a cucumber.

"We need to talk about this divorce, George," I said.

"No we don't," he shot back. "You're my wife forever. Until the day I die."

My heart sank because I just knew how unreasonable he was. It was true, he wasn't going to go anywhere without a fight. And I wasn't sure I had the fight left in me.

He looked at me, sensing my unease. "But don't worry Kerry – because I *will* die."

George had been going to spiritualist churches and getting lots of medium and psychic readings, I wonder if that had had an effect on his mindset.

"Shut up, stupid, you're not going to die," I told him.

"I am," he said.

Looking back now, how prophetic were those words? He was absolutely right. He was convinced he was going to die and he did. But of course at the time it was just more threats.

It was terrifying yet tedious and I just hoped, somehow, we could get a clean divorce and move on with our lives.

Over the next few weeks things quietened down. Being without George and learning to live without the constant threat of violence gave me a renewed energy. I threw myself into panto at Christmas, trying to make enough money to feed the kids and moved in with my mate Ampika Pickston, the star of The Real Housewives of Cheshire. I was so grateful for her generosity and friendship. It was helpful to have a safe haven near Manchester, where I was performing, and knowing my kids could be with me.

George stayed relatively calm, although we did have a couple of instances where the police would be called to oversee the handover when he came to pick up DJ for his parental visits.

One time he simply wouldn't leave Ampika's property so we called them out. He was being threatening and kicking off, claiming we were taking too long to bring him DJ. In the end DJ barely stayed five minutes with him. He ended up bringing her straight back because she was becoming so distressed and didn't want to see him.

It must have hurt him, but he did the right thing in bringing her back.

At this point I was still convinced he wouldn't ever hurt her.

But things were about to get really tricky, when George started to make real, sinister threats to her safety.

It was March 2018, almost a year after the roof incident and our 'final' break-up and I was getting on with my life. As I said, we had hooked up a couple of times, but that had all ended in the previous November. I was slowly starting to come out the other side, trying to figure it all out now I was out of his bed. I was finally feeling strong. As far as the general public knew, we were officially over and those divorce papers were in his hands.

I even did a lovely shoot with all the kids for OK! magazine, to talk about moving on from the marriage. They ran my quote on the front page, the headline big and bold alongside a beautiful picture of me, Molly, Lilly, Max, Heidi and DJ. "We're happier now," it said. "I wouldn't take George back in a million years."

I meant it. But don't forget he was the father of my child and for all George's terrible, terrible faults, I wanted her to have a daddy more than I wanted to be completely free of him. But there was always that little voice in the back of my head, the fear that he could do something to her, take her, keep her, hurt her to get back at me.

Things came to a head on Mother's Day.

In what proved to be a turning point, one which, for me, truly altered the course of all our lives, I made the decision to take out a restraining order against him.

It was an action that wasn't taken lightly, but which sparked a series of events that eventually left me so low I became suicidal. Yes, I'm looking at you Fathers 4 Justice, but I'll get to that.

I've no doubt my decision to legally stop George from coming near us further contributed to the mental decline that resulted in his death, but I was no longer prepared to risk my family's safety when he was continuously proving to be a danger to himself and the kids. NO chance.

It was a beautiful spring day. I must have been feeling fairly happy and comfortable with where we were at because I Facetimed George, so he could speak to DJ. It just so happened on that day, DJ, being a three-year-old, wasn't in the mood to chat. She was a toddler, she was distracted and didn't want to sit and talk. It was nothing personal against her father, she was just a baby!

But when she refused to engage with him, George didn't see it like that. Of course he saw it as me turning her against him.

His big smile at seeing his daughter very quickly twisted into a scowl. Darkness fell across his face as he glared at his quiet little girl. "I see," he snarled.

# Time's Up

Oh God, I knew where this was going immediately. Even though he was miles away, trapped inside a tiny iPad screen, unable to get to us, I felt those all too familiar knots in my stomach as I watched his face change. It was a look I'd seen so many times before, but somehow this felt different. This felt directed at DJ and I was more frightened than I'd ever been in my life.

He turned his attention back to me, partly to my relief. "I read your fucking magazine article. You think you're so clever don't ya?" he spat into the camera.

I was taken aback by the sheer vitriol, but not surprised. Of course he was pissed off by the interview. I should have known it would trigger an irrational rage. I'd publicly stated in a best-selling, national magazine that I was happier without him. That I didn't need him. Of course this was going to push all his buttons, his ego would have been battered by this.

"What are you on about George?" I pleaded, despite knowing full well what his issue was.

His eyes narrowed. "Watch what happens next, Kerry."

I froze. "George, what are you talking about?"

Tiny, innocent DJ, previously uninterested, now sensed the shift in tone. Sat with me, her intuitive little brain must have noticed the sudden fear sucking the life from the room, and she was now all wide eyes on the screen, watching her father.

"DJ, hold on tight to your fucking mother, I'm fucking coming to get you." His threatening tone and the use of language in front of our child scared and riled me in equal measure. "George! Don't talk to her like that, she's three for God's sake!"

Again, staring straight at DJ he repeated his earlier threat, almost so quiet it was a whisper.

"Watch what fucking happens now."

"George, that'll do now…"

He interrupted me. "Wait and see, Kerry. Just you watch. She can die with me."

I could barely breathe. How could he be saying such things? He was talking like a mad man, threatening to kill his child? He must be on something.

He looked again at DJ. "Daddy's coming for you."

Suddenly those black, empty eyes turned back to me. It was like seeing a devil come to life.

"How's your mum, Kerry?" he smirked. "Is she alright?"

I felt my blood run cold. Oh please, no. My brain was racing. Please don't hurt DJ. Or my mum. Come for me, I don't care, but don't lay a finger on my family. The silent pleas ran through my mind as my body went into panic mode. I was unable to speak, gripped in icy fear.

For a third time he uttered his now terrifyingly familiar mantra, "You just watch what happens." He winked, and hung up.

I sat there, glued to the spot, staring at a now blank screen, for what seemed like an eternity. Even our DJ was dead still, knowing something had changed, knowing a threat had been made that could never be taken back.

George's sinister wink at the end of the call scared me far more than getting a good hiding. At least when he was beating me up I knew what I was getting. But now, in this situation, I didn't know what he was going to do next. One minute his face filled the iPad screen, then, in the blink of an eye, he was gone, like a magician in a puff of smoke. It was chilling. What *was* coming next? Was he coming for me? My mum? For DJ?

# Time's Up

I was shaking like a leaf, but trying hard not to let DJ see how scared I was. And then, just like that, the magician was back. I heard a familiar 'ding' as the email icon in the corner of my screen flashed up. It was a message from George.

Written in a tone that I knew full well was designed to manipulate and frighten, but which to the outside eye would seem concerned and almost caring, the message was chilling. He was planning something. Gathering written evidence to use against me. It was so calculating, so… evil… I almost lost my breath reading it aloud.

*"Kerry, why have you hung up when I was having a nice conversation with my daughter?"* it said. *"Have you been taking your medication properly? Are you drinking again? I'll speak to my lawyer about this."*

To me that email was the final nail in the coffin. This could well be the most manipulative thing he'd done to date. How could he change so quickly? Lie so easily? It was at that moment I reached for the telephone and with shaking hands called the police to tell them everything and request a restraining order against my husband.

They gave it to me immediately.

*****

Despite not actually having heard of a support group called Fathers 4 Justice at this point, I understand now that in the days following that call, George, fuelled by rage and armed with fake ammunition in the form of his made-up emails, had reached out to them.

They're a so-called human rights organisation who fight for

divorced or separated dads to get proper access to their kids. Now don't get me wrong, I think anything like that is a fantastic cause, I'm a firm believer, having been a single mum for the majority of my kids' lives, that fathers should be involved with their children.

But *not* the fathers who are proving to be a danger to their families. It makes no sense to me why you'd want to give a violent man access to a child just because he sees it as 'his right'. I get some mums do the wrong thing and deny access out of spite, but you can't always take the man's word in a situation like that. There are always two sides to every story.

Anyway, it was obvious George was liaising with F4J because once he died, Matt O'Connor, the founder of the bloody thing, printed a load of nonsense on their website that still exists there to this day.

Without ever coming to me for a right of reply, they reprinted lies that George had told them, with no evidence whatsoever. And of course this would be from the time that I'd put a restraining order on him for threatening the life of his own daughter. I bet he never told you that part, did he Matt?

Loud and proud on the website, Matt had written the following slurs:

– *George told me he was DJ's primary carer much of the time when Kerry was on drink and drug benders, or away on publicised 'holidays' organised by her agent.*

Not true. As if George would let me leave the house most of the time! Do you think I could go anywhere?! There were times I'd have to travel for work, and that was to pay the bills, because George wasn't working!

– *He said there was an abusive pattern to Kerry's behaviour.*

The abuser makes out he is the one being abused. Again, Not true.

*– He said Kerry thought kids equalled cash, and she had a history of denying her children access to their fathers having done the same to her ex, Mark Croft.*

Go track down Mark Croft yourself and see if he was in the slightest bit bothered about supporting his children. Not true. My kids are my world, not the contents of my wallet.

*– He begged and begged Kerry and her solicitors for contact with his daughter but was repeatedly denied any kind of access, including supervised contact.*

I imagine you'd do the same Matt, if your baby mama had threatened to kill your child.

What Matt and these Fathers 4 Justice don't realise is just how scared I was that George would hurt DJ. That he had manipulated them into believing his warped narrative – because that's what abusers do.

I don't want DJ to read this one day and think her daddy didn't love her, because he did. But once he'd gone past the point of any rationality, it was clear he couldn't be trusted to be alone with her. He was so poorly by that point.

I remember once, before I took out the restraining order, when George had DJ for a couple of days. I was already uneasy about it but seeing as he was her dad, and unlike what F4J would have you believe, I agreed to let them have the time together.

As I was going about my business I heard a report on the radio that a young father had jumped from a bridge with his three-year-old, killing them both. Don't ask me why, with all the millions of people in the country it could've been, but I almost had a heart attack thinking it was George and DJ.

It was irrational on my part but with shaking hands I dialled his number and was flooded with relief when he answered the phone and I heard their voices. My baby was safe.

But imagine having to feel like that every time your child goes to see her dad. On tenterhooks and living in fear that he could have a bad day or a funny turn and next thing you know, they're both gone.

The first time I'd actually ever heard of F4J was after George died, which is still the most painful topic to discuss, but I'll get to it.

The very next day, in the aftermath of one of the most shocking things that's ever happened in my life, I got a call from my then manager, Paul.

"Kerry, I don't want to do this but I thought you needed to know. You're being publicly blamed for George's death," he said.

My blood ran cold. Armed with the information Paul gave me, I went straight onto Twitter where F4J were spitting vitriol. Telling people George was dead because I'd refused to let him see his daughter, like they knew even half the story! His body wasn't even cold, in fact I was on my way to the Chapel of Rest to see him at that very moment! I was still in a state of complete and utter shock and they were taking to social media to do this to me?!

My grief and surprise gave way to anger. How dare they?! What would people say if I knew George had threatened to harm DJ, and yet I'd still handed her over to him? What kind of mum would that have made me?! This so called protest group, who in my opinion give loving fathers seeking real justice a bad name, went on to call me a murderer, saying I had blood on my hands, telling me and the world I should be locked up.

Apparently my kids needed to be taken off me because George had died.

Oh, how I wanted to scream from the rooftops: "Do you not know how many times I tried to save that man? I already have such guilt that he died!"

But even now I will stand on George's grave, put my hand on my heart and stick by the decisions I made to protect my daughter. The restraining order, the solicitors, the supervised visits, all of it. In fact the restraining order had been up for four months by the time he'd died and he hadn't even once tried to contact me or DJ.

George was so troubled. Nothing was stopping him getting help and turning his life around the way I did. Nothing. But he wasn't strong enough. No matter what anyone says, it was not my fault he died alone in that hotel room, begging for friends. I didn't put those drugs in his hand.

So for F4J to do that to me, at my lowest ebb, without any of the facts, was unforgivable. And not just to me, but to the kids too. To know DJ could read those slurs one day, was too much to bear. Molly and Lilly were so incensed they took to Twitter to defend me, knowing full well what we'd been through as a family with George.

F4J's attacks left me in such a bad way that the doctor had to come out to administer an injection just to calm me down. I felt sure in that moment I was headed for a breakdown. I even contemplated suicide. I was that bad.

Would the public really believe what Matt and F4J were saying about me? As my husband lay dead in a chapel, would the papers truly think it was me who put him there?

Like a fool I read a lot of the comments from other Twitter

users who blindly sided with F4J. The word 'murderer' came up a lot. 'You'll pay!' some keyboard warrior spat from behind the safety of their mobile phone screen.

I hadn't had that sort of negative attention since I was with Mark Croft. I'd kept myself clean and sorted myself out and yet here I was, back there, through no fault of my own.

My head was so messed up at this point it's a wonder I was able to come through it.

Not only did I have to deal with the confusing, shocking nature of George's death, I was also torn between feeling guilt, responsibility and sheer confusion for something that genuinely wasn't my fault.

Of course, F4J didn't see any of that. All they saw were some made up emails from George designed to set me up. But I can't worry about that now.

I would never ever stop my kids from seeing their dads. Not even Mark Croft. It's just he's not made an attempt. Brian still sees Molly and Lilly. So why would I have ever tried to stop George? I'll tell you why F4J – because George was violent, he was controlling, he was scary. He threatened to rape my mum. He told me people armed with machetes were coming to blow the house up and in the same breath asked if I could bring DJ round.

I know George was very charming, endearing, manipulative and convincing. So part of me understands why they were taken in by him – but, like I said before, there's always two sides to every story!

And I have my truth, which F4J never once cared to hear.

For them to go ahead and print those lies, with no basis other than the fact they Googled my past drug abuse and bankruptcy, neither of which had anything to do with George or his death, was pure evil. They literally wrote that I'd murdered George! Even now I worry about DJ seeing that. My little girl could one day read that pile of nonsense on the F4J website and think Mummy killed Daddy.

I wanted to get my lawyers involved, but of course at that point I didn't have the money.

I was a mess at that time. It was an absolute nightmare.

And yes, it did make me question myself. People think I killed George. Well, did I?

Did he do this intentionally because of me?! I believe the truth is George was too vain to kill himself deliberately. And the inquest proved that. It was accidental. It wasn't supposed to happen.

*****

It was 16 months after I was awarded the restraining order against George when he was found lying on the dirty carpet of a Holiday Inn, just hours from death.

In the interim I pushed ahead with the divorce, now fully free of him thanks to said restraining order. Although as predicted, he made it as difficult for me as possible.

I couldn't afford a lawyer so Danielle Brown acted as my McKenzie friend, my representative at the divorce hearings.

And, of course, George being George couldn't allow that! He told the court it would be unfair having Danielle there – because he'd been sleeping with her!

Now luckily I know Danielle so well and I trust her with my life, she's my best friend in the world and the thought didn't even cross my mind that George would be telling the truth. He was a fool though – here he was, trying to get money and spousal support off me, knowing I didn't have a penny to my name, but yet telling a judge HE was the one having an affair. At what point did he think he'd win his case if everyone thought HE was a cheater? He clearly didn't think that one through.

I remember listening to him in court, via a video link, casually tell the judge about this so-called affair. Danielle and I looked at each other and our mouths dropped open in pure shock. I couldn't believe what I was hearing.

Danielle looked scared, because in that moment I think she realised the full extent of George's problems. The fact he lied so easily, she was dumbfounded, to the point she actually started laughing in disbelief.

Well you had to laugh, really. It was all so absurd, he was behaving so oddly, it was actually funny. He wanted me to be there by myself, scared, alone, weak to prove how powerful he was. Having Danielle by my side made me strong, and he knew that.

And he hated it.

I had to laugh at some of George's demands too. He'd convinced lawyers to represent him on the promise that I was somehow loaded and they could all expect a big ol' pay day when they won. To this day I have no idea how he actually paid them for their services.

Anyway, he wanted £8k for tattoo removal. He wanted private holidays, as he couldn't risk travelling publicly 'being in the public eye'. He kept telling lawyers and such he just wanted 'his half' – but yet he knew full well I didn't have any cash. I'd initially wanted to get a divorce online for £500! And at the time that in itself was a hell of a lot!

Was he trying to bankrupt me again? Or was he genuinely confused? Or did he just keep telling himself I had money to the point he believed it himself?

Either way he never got his cash. Because we never did make it to the divorce. He simply stopped turning up to the hearings and refused to acknowledge it was even happening. What could I do? When he died, we were technically still married. I'm still, to this day, a widow.

He only went to two hearings. On the day he lied about his affair, I went to an OK! magazine party later that night. I wore a red dress and a wig and Danielle came with me. I remember her telling me in the car on the way there, "I'll never get married." She'd seen the shit show that was mine and George's marriage and she was having none of it.

How I made it to the party that night, I don't know. I was emotionally drained. But it was almost a release to go out and just laugh for a change. But look closely at those photos and you could see I wasn't right.

Meanwhile George was trying to capitalise on the split by going around telling people he was filming a new reality show called 'Life After Kerry'. Which was total and utter nonsense.

It breaks my heart now to think of how different everything could've been if we'd just stayed amicable and George had played ball.

Could a clean divorce have given him the opportunity to move on with his life, get the help he needed and start again? Rather than cling to his association with me in the most pathetic way?

It still haunts me to this day, yet after the restraining order, we didn't see each other again.

*****

In 2018 I was up north, doing panto in Northwich, which is near to where George was living with his parents. I was alone up there, staying in a little cottage, every second of every day shitting myself that he'd find me.

I heard rumours he was threatening to come to the panto, armed with a knife and was planning to pull me off stage and kill me there and then because I wouldn't let him see DJ.

Luckily he never showed up but I was so scared he'd find me. Every night on stage I was on edge, I could barely focus. Even though George wasn't in my life anymore, he still loomed so large. I was always so, so terrified he'd show up again.

After he died, my worst instincts were confirmed. One of his friends came round and told me I'd done the right thing in keeping him away from DJ. Apparently he'd planned on injecting her with heroin and then killing himself. Have you ever heard anything more horrifying?! My whole body went cold when I was told. But in that moment, I knew without a shadow of a doubt, I'd done the right thing in leaving him forever.

His mate also told me about how George went out and got himself blue contact lenses. She said he planned on finding DJ to show her that his "eyes had turned blue just like hers, because he missed her so much." To anyone else it might've been a sweet gesture, but with George it was nothing but sinister.

I was never, ever at ease in that last year of his life. I was always looking over my shoulder, catching my breath and praying he wouldn't show up, before one day he just went ahead and died, his stomach full of coke.

But before that tragedy ripped my world apart, an unexpected angel came into my life and changed everything, forever.

# 9

## Ryan

I met Ryan on Bumble, which was one of the newer dating apps in 2018. Danielle made me go on it. I don't think I'd been on a date in about a year or so, after the Mike/pregnancy debacle, and she was ready for me to have some fun again, even if I wasn't.

With George out of the picture, I was now on a mission of self love. I was done with men and drama and instead I wanted to focus on myself. Those months alone were so, so important in shaping me, after everything I'd been through. I was learning to be independent again, to love myself. The kids saw such a difference in me and I was feeling stronger and happier than I'd done in a while. It had taken work to get to that point – self acceptance, prayers, healing, and looking after myself to the best of my abilities, and I was finally in a really good place.

And to be honest, the thought of being in a relationship actually made me feel sick. George had done such a number on me, that it meant I was in no rush to jump into something new.

But I was down south, by myself, living alone with just the

kids and although I was feeling great, there were points where the loneliness was unbearable.

There were some days I longed for adult company. Maybe Danielle had a point. Dating could be a fun distraction. Neither of us thought for a second I'd end up meeting husband number four!

When I first saw Ryan's picture on the app, the one thing I noticed were his eyes. They were kind. There was something really sweet about him, which, as you'll know, is so not the type I'd normally go for. I've always liked a dangerous bad boy and from the off I could see that wasn't Ryan's vibe, even in his pictures.

But you know what? If you keep going for the same guy, you'll end up with the same results. And I couldn't bear to have another George or Mark Croft on my hands.

Before I could talk myself out of it, I thought: 'What the hell'. I hadn't heard from George thanks to the restraining order and I'd heard on the grapevine he had girlfriends of his own, so I'd figured he'd leave me to it.

I really had nothing to lose – plus I could get a free meal out of it! Who doesn't love a freebie?!

With Bumble the woman has to message the lad first, so I did actually have to be proactive. It went against every fibre of my being to message Ryan, I was nervous, unsure, doubtful, but something inside pushed me. *It's only a bit of fun, Kerry.*

So I sent him a simple message. "Hi!"

After a bit of small talk on the app, we swapped details and planned to meet for lunch.

We'd arranged for him to pick me up in his Golf at about 2pm on an ordinary Friday afternoon and he was late coming to collect me. That's something I've since learnt is the norm for him. The man has no concept of time!

When he did eventually turn up I was struck by how sweet he looked. He was the polar opposite to George in stature and appearance. He was a different kind of handsome. He was younger than me too, by eight years.

We went to the White Hart pub and ordered sea bass – and then I proceeded to interview him. I basically fired a load of questions at him as if I was Alan Sugar on The Apprentice.

I don't know what came over me, but I wasn't being particularly flirty, or even that charming, I just wanted to know what his deal was.

One of the questions I asked him, genuinely, was: "Where do you see yourself in five years' time?"

He replied, "I'll be a millionaire."

Well that caught my attention. I'd heard comments like that before from the likes of George and Mark, and I knew the source of their fictional wealth would always be dodgy. Drugs, unsavoury dealings, etc. They were bad boys who thought they could make a living above the law.

But Ryan was straight down the line. I could see that immediately.

Right from the off he was incredibly ambitious and driven. He knew what he wanted when it came to business and at that point he was working on starting up a gym brand. He was so proud of it and told me all about the marketing, trying to promote it and stuff. It was refreshing to hear someone be so passionate about something so… normal.

Everything about him was perfect on paper. He was nice. He was safe. He was a *good guy*.

**Looking to the future**
It's been a hell of a rollercoaster ride over the past ten years, but I've taken control of my life again and I feel better than ever

**It started here** Happy school days in Warrington. Pictured above with Carrie, Kelly and Louise. I never dreamt my life would end up the way it has, it's been some journey

**Reaching for the big time** The original Kittens – me with Liz McClarnon and Natasha Hamilton launching the band in Liverpool 24 years ago. Where did the time go?

**Aunty Angela** She was more than my aunty, she was a sister to me. There was only ten years between us

**Miss you, Nan Betty** I fell on the floor screaming and crying when I was told she had died – I was inconsolable

**Thanks Mum** Celebrating my mum Sue's 60th birthday. Without the childhood I had, I wouldn't be the person I am today

**Gorgeous George** Hearing George joke about prison turned me on

**Dreamy Dubai** I still look back on pictures from that holiday – it felt perfect

**A new family** Early days with DJ. George was doing everything, he never left my side

**Two different people** The drugs clearly didn't agree with George but he carried on

**Softer side** With my nan and mum. When my nan died he really stepped up for me

**Smile for the camera** George, Liz, Natasha and me, expecting DJ

♡

*Always in my heart*

**You are my world** I am so proud of my beautiful children, they are the best thing that has ever happened to me. I love them so much. (Clockwise, from top) Max, Heidi and DJ; Molly, DJ and Lilly; Max, Heidi and DJ and the girls together on a pyjama night

**First picture** A selfie with a new man I am dating – I met Ryan on Bumble

**Romantic Rome** It was a slow burner with Ryan but I've never looked back

**I do** Showing off my engagement ring after Ryan popped the question. And my family were with me (right) to share the moment

**My best friend**
With Danielle and her baby bump. I wish she had been in my life from the start, she's bloody perfect!

**Big Reunion** Back with the Kittens again. I jumped at the chance to rejoin the band in 2012 but I felt like I struggled to fit in at times and it wouldn't last

**Girls night out** With Lesley, Dawn and Lilly. Dawn has been a lifesaver for me and my family and I love our Lesley, and Lilly of course

**Life begins at 40** With Molly and Lilly, celebrating a big birthday in style

**Sealed with a kiss** Never before has a man changed my life in the way Ryan has. I can take on the world… and then some

**Why not?** I unapologetically make a mint showing off my body on subscription website OnlyFans

**Happy holidays** We're a stronger family than we've ever been. My kids are the ones I graft to provide for. My only goal in life now is to be the best parent I can be

# Ryan

In other words, he wasn't for me.

You see, with Ryan it was a real slow burner. I was impressed by his ambition, and there was no doubt I fancied him, he's gorgeous to look at. But in those initial stages I was absolutely terrified of getting into another relationship. I loved being in his company, but I wasn't blown away. Of course I know now that in many cases this is a much healthier way to start a relationship. Don't jump in quickly, get to know one another. There's no need to rush things.

And still, something in me was intrigued and when he asked me out again, I said yes. And again after that, until suddenly we were dating regularly.

For me it was important to keep the pace slow. I was enjoying being around Ryan but he didn't meet the kids for at least three months and that was a deliberate decision on my part. I wanted to be sure of him.

It was around this time, in late 2018, that I got a call about a possible appearance on Celebs Go Dating, a brilliant E4 show that sets up celebs on dates and sticks them in front of psychologists to determine why they're still single. Despite its rather serious sounding premise, it's hilarious and perfect fodder for someone like me. It doesn't take itself too seriously, millions of people watch it, and, more than anything, the money they paid was decent.

At the time no one outside of my inner circle knew just how serious things were getting with Ryan. The press reported we were 'casually dating' but I'd deliberately kept him out of the spotlight as much as possible, and he certainly preferred it that way too. He's one of those people who pays no mind to showbiz news and gossip. When we first met he admitted to recognising me, but he had no idea about my past or why I was famous. It was weirdly refreshing and felt like a clean slate, to be with someone who had absolutely no interest in fame at all.

So as far as everyone was aware, I was single and ready to mingle.

The truth is, I had started to fall in love with Ryan. I realised it when I was away on a bootcamp in Marbella and I felt this strange sensation in my stomach, having been gone from home for a few days.

"I miss the guy," I said aloud to no one in particular. I wanted to be with him. We'd been together only a few months at this point, but I couldn't ignore that my feelings for him were getting stronger.

So it really did throw a bit of a spanner in the works when Celebs Go Dating approached me.

My manager, Paul, had left me feeling as if nobody wanted to work with me but n hindsight I think it was him who just didn't want to work for me any longer..

But 'Dating' was different. They saw something in me that they knew would be TV gold and they took a chance. I was so broke at this point I was practically salivating to do it, despite the change in my personal life.

Ryan and I were in Thailand on a break when the producers called to tell me I was in. We were on a working holiday of sorts, hence why I could afford to be there. I had set up some pap pictures which I knew would net me a bit of cash – I was at the stage in my career and life where the paparazzi provided one of the very few means I had of making money.

I got off the phone.

"Ryan, I got the Celebs Go Dating gig!" I squealed, trying to sound super excited in the naive hope he might feel the same. His poor face went as white as a sheet. I could tell immediately he was gutted. I suppose anyone would be, if they were sending their other half off on dates with a bunch of handsome strangers. It would truly be a huge early test for our brand new relationship.

"I promise darling, nothing will happen," I said quickly, sensing how uneasy he was. "I'm treating it like an acting job. It's not real. I'd never actually do anything with anyone on telly. Besides, my kids would kill me if I did!"

I knew he would come around, but he's such a deep thinker, it took him a little while. Molly, on the other hand, was very vocal about not wanting me to do it.

"Oh my God! I can't bear the thought of you with your tongue down someone's throat on TV, Mum!" She yelped down the phone. "You're too old!"

The cheek!

For me, the idea of getting back on telly and getting a good pay packet to boot was far more attractive than the format of the show itself. I would never have embarrassed my kids in that respect anyway, with or without Ryan being on the scene. The thought of being intimate with a bloke on the first date – on camera – with my children watching at home? I couldn't bear it. I'm a bit of a prude in that respect. Yes, I do OnlyFans, but that doesn't involve being physical with anyone. I get shy quite easily, believe it or not.

Ryan eventually sat me down. He'd been brooding on it a lot.

"Listen," he said gently. "I'm not going to stop you going out there and making money for your babies. Just make sure you come back home to me every night, ok?"

I was relieved. It was such a sweet thing to say and it proved he wasn't the possessive, jealous type. George wouldn't have even allowed me to take the initial call, let alone agree to be on the show. But yet here was Ryan, telling me to go out and graft for my family, even if it did mean hiding our true relationship a while longer.

It turns out there was more to the show than just the dating. Working with the dating experts, Paul Carrick Brunson and Anna Williamson, was actually an incredibly emotional experience. The tears I cried were real. The deep dive into my past was real. All the emotions were true and the process started to become less about finding a lover and more about finding myself.

Suddenly it wasn't the dating aspect that threatened to derail my new relationship, it was the realisation that perhaps I really did need to be on my own for a little while longer.

And so, a week after filming finished, I ended things with Ryan.

He had kind of moved in during production, he was helping to babysit the kids, while I was out being filmed on dates. It takes a certain kind of man to do that – but I think it freaked me out. Having been working on myself so much, I was beginning to feel like I needed to be independent again. I took the therapy element of the show incredibly seriously.

Ryan was devastated. And I was too to an extent but I really believed it was the right decision. I had become dead scared and panicky. I'd convinced myself he was too nice, he wasn't the one, I shouldn't be in a relationship, I keep ruining my kids lives by bringing these men in. I needed to concentrate on the children now.

Two weeks later and I was sat in a quiet house. Molly was

away, Lilly was out with her friends, Max was in his room, Heidi was watching TV in the living room with DJ and I was sat there on my own. I suddenly started to question myself. Why had I given up a good man to focus on my kids, when my kids were growing up and didn't need me as much? And actually – having Ryan there never really distracted me from them anyway! They were always my priority.

I started to realise I *could* have it both ways.

As I sat there I desperately missed Ryan. Just the comfort of having him near me, the safety of knowing he was there. I'd never experienced that before. He wasn't a clown like Brian, or an enabler like Mark, or an abusive person like George. He represented a new kind of love, one that took me a long time to appreciate, but one that now I don't think I could live without.

We got back together barely a fortnight after I'd called it off. I had to apologise and let him know where my head was at, and, Ryan being Ryan, took it all in his stride and totally understood my point of view.

He obviously really loved me.

*****

I had told him about George and the abuse right from the start. Not as a means to scare him off, but rather just to be completely honest. Ryan had even dropped me off at one of the divorce proceedings that George never turned up for. That's the sort of guy he is. An angel.

There was so much baggage attached to me at that point – the split, the restraining order, all the previous trauma.

People have since asked me, "Was Ryan not put off by your

history and all the drama?" and I used to ask myself that question too. But I had to change my mindset. Every family has drama and every story has its ups and downs. And any man that comes into my life should consider themselves so lucky, because me and my kids are ace. We're absolutely awesome. There's no place here for anyone who feels my children or my past are a burden.

Mark Croft used to taunt me all the time after we split, telling me, "Who the hell would want you, used up with four kids?"

George would say the same sort of thing during our many break-ups. It took a lot to make me change my perspective, but I know now that every single family has their problems. And that's life.

I'll continue to have drama as the kids get older, when they start bringing their own grown up issues to the door. But you know what? That's fine. And Ryan knows that. He just gets it.

Ryan was the first guy I've ever been with who truly understood me.

I remember I sat him down and told him things about my childhood, the abuse with George, and he simply said, "I'm so sorry you were made to feel like that."

That blew me away. No man had ever said that to me before. No man had ever apologised on behalf of another for making me feel like shit about myself.

Another time, when I was really poorly suffering from a tummy bug, Ryan left work early to come and look after me, and brought a brand new pair of trainers for me to cheer me up.

I couldn't believe it, he'd bought me something with his own money! He'd taken time off work, just to care for me! He was always so, so generous with his money and his time and he really proved himself.

# Ryan

He was also soft and gentle with the children, which impressed me. He really took his time – and he had a lot to contend with!

Molly was awful to Ryan at the beginning and although they're best friends now, it took a while. I understand why she was reluctant, having seen everything I'd been through with Mark and George, but she was sometimes unnecessarily mean to him. DJ as well, was very wary of him. She's one of those children who needs you to earn their trust at the best of times. She won't give you a smile unless you really work for it. And of course, having not seen her dad for a while at this point, she was probably extra sceptical of this new man who seemed to be around all the time. It was a lot for her little mind to process. But he was amazing with her.

Even my dog Paddy kicked off when Ryan was around. It's like he became particularly protective of me, he'd bark and snap when Ryan would hold my hand.

In many ways it was touching to see my family have my back – and even better seeing how Ryan handled it all so patiently.

But the true test of our relationship was to come just a few short months later. If our mini split and my kids' contempt hadn't managed to put Ryan off, the huge tragedy we were about to face could well have been the nail in the coffin.

Just as I had gained one significant man in my life, I was about to lose another, in the most unthinkable way.

# 10

# The End

George wasn't meant for this earth.

I know that now. He was put here for a reason and that was to give me DJ. I believe that in my heart and hold on to it even now, years after his death. It brings me some sort of peace.

But on the day I found out he'd perished, slipping away on the floor of the Runcorn Holiday Inn, shortly after he was seen begging for friends, there was no peace to be found. At all.

It was Saturday 6 July, 2019. I hadn't spoken to George in a year. Having met Ryan, I had completely moved on from him and it had made things easier in a lot of ways, as the kids had got used to George not being around as a result. At last, there was no more back and forths, no more splitting and reuniting, things seemed… stable.

Of course I was still terrified of seeing George out and about, especially as the restraining order had expired four months previously. We hadn't heard anything from him, but still I was on the edge, and wondering even then what he was capable of. But with Ryan by my side I felt a renewed strength.

# The End

On that awful day I was headed to Harley Street with Ryan, seeing a doctor for some sort of vanity procedure or consultation, I forget now but knowing me it was probably to do with my boobs.

As we pulled up outside, my phone rang. It was George's dad, calling via Facetime. I started shaking. I can't explain it but I knew full well something was wrong. With the restraining order no longer in place, there was nothing stopping him turning up at my house to cause trouble.

And there would be no reason for his dad to be calling unless it was bad news. Every instinct in my body told me to panic.

I never said a word to Ryan, I just put the ringing phone back in my bag and ignored it. Maybe if I completely detached myself from the situation, buried my head in the sand, the whole thing would just disappear. No phone call, no problem.

I walked into the surgery trying to be my normal, bubbly self, but my heart was in my mouth. Of course I couldn't just ignore it. Why was his dad trying to ring me now, after all this time? Suddenly dark thoughts started racing through my mind. This must mean George is on one. Has he got DJ?! Is he anywhere near my kids?

I sat through the consultation in a daze before hastily wrapping it up so I could get out of there. I'm not sure if Ryan clocked my unease or not, but if he did he didn't say so at the time. Afterwards we got back in the car and my phone rang again. It was George's dad.

Oh Christ.

"Ryan, George's dad is trying to ring me, what's going on?" I spluttered.

Ryan couldn't offer an explanation any more than I could and just seemed perplexed that I wasn't answering. But I needed to keep the phone line free. I needed to speak to the kids. I didn't want to face whatever information George's dad had to tell me.

Unforeseen panic started to rise in my throat as I called home. All five children were there, Molly and Lilly were looking after the little ones.

Lilly answered.

"Lock the door," I said.

"Why?! What's going on?" she replied.

"Just do it now, please. George's dad's ringing me and I'm worried he might be down south. So just do what I say."

Lilly didn't argue, she agreed she'd lock up and came off the phone.

My breathing was getting heavier – there was nothing to stop him going to the house, or trying to take DJ. The kids would be powerless if he turned up!

The phone rang again. It was my then-manager, Paul.

I can't explain it, but suddenly it dawned on me. I just knew. My heart sunk. I turned to Ryan as the phone buzzed in my hand.

"George's dead," I said.

"What are you on about?" Ryan was always calm, no matter what. "It's probably George himself calling you now to wind you up. He's probably on one, it's the weekend."

"It's not George, Ryan, it's Paul."

I answered the phone.

Paul spoke first. "Kerry, darling, where are you?"

I didn't even bother to answer. "You're calling me to tell me George is dead, aren't you?"

He paused. "I am, love. He's gone."

# The End

It was the most bizarre thing in the world. I just knew. And I didn't even need Paul to tell me how it had happened. My gut instinct said it was drugs. Either that or he was murdered thanks to the amount of money he owed.

But it didn't stop me screaming. I screamed and cried as a shocked Ryan, my relatively new boyfriend, held me in his arms.

I couldn't believe it. I thought if I knew George was gone forever the fear would go too – but I was now more frightened than ever.

My first thought was: how the hell was I going to tell the children? And in particular, how was I going to tell my five-year-old her daddy is dead?! My heart ached for DJ and for George, who would now never have the chance to meet again. But Ryan, he kept on holding me. Who does that? Who consoles a girlfriend as she weeps over the death of her estranged husband? It was a sign of what a good man Ryan was.

It turns out George had died after eating a ball of cocaine he'd stashed in a sock. After everything he'd been through, that was the way he went out.

He had been staying at the Holiday Inn for a few days and was taking so many drugs that he had been hallucinating, telling staff there that he was seeing wasps and shadows in his room. Police were apparently called a few hours before his death after fellow guests complained he'd been wandering the hotel corridors asking them to be his friend. They saw the drugs in his room and they knew full well he wasn't right. He kept telling them he was troubled, that he was having problems in his personal life and freely admitted to snorting the cocaine.

Later, at the inquest, the police officer admitted she wasn't worried about the drugs and didn't feel there was enough to arrest him for possession, but she was mainly concerned for his welfare.

If they'd arrested him or brought him to a hospital that night I'm sure he would still be alive today. Instead, when housekeeping came to the room the next morning, along with some hotel staff, George was sat there eating the drugs from the sock.

He quickly became unwell, an ambulance was called but he died shortly after at the hospital. And that was the end of his story.

Mental illness and drugs had finally taken him.

As I said, my main fear as Ryan and I made the long, horrific car journey home from Harley Street that day was how on earth I would break the news to the kids, especially DJ.

I know she hadn't seen George for a year at this point, but now, the reality was, she'd never ever have the option to see him again. And that brought with it such a sense of guilt, even though I knew I did the right thing in stopping their contact. I never wanted DJ growing up and witnessing those drug-fuelled episodes – and George was showing no sign of getting the help he truly needed. I had offered supervised visits but I pulled one at the last minute as I knew if he wanted to just get up and take DJ, nothing would stop him. I later found out from a friend of his that George had actually been to the visiting centre to scope it out, to see how he could leave with her without getting stopped. He probably thought he was above the law or something.

But now he was gone for good there was absolutely no chance of redemption whatsoever.

We got home and I asked Ryan if he could take DJ to Morrison's. I needed to speak to the kids and I didn't want DJ's reaction to mimic her older sisters and brother. She was at the age when she was copying them a lot. I needed to speak to her separately.

So Ryan took DJ, and I sat in the living room, with the other kids gathered around me.

"What's the matter, Mum? What's happened?" Lilly asked.

I tried to be as gentle as I could.

"I'm so sorry to tell you this, kids," I said. "But George died today."

There was a hushed silence, almost eerie, but then both Max and Heidi threw themselves to the floor, bursting into tears and wailing.

Molly was still. She never cried – not in that moment or since. I don't think she's shed one tear over George. And Lilly was just shocked. She was all over the place, in fact. I thought she'd throw her arms around me and comfort me, like the Lilly I know. But she didn't. She backed away. I think she internalised things, or maybe she was just at the age where she was acting a bit more selfishly. Either way, her reaction was unexpected. She left the room, while I tried to console Max and Heidi with Molly's help, as my own emotions went wild.

*****

A little while later DJ came home with Ryan, stocked up with new toys from the shop. Bless Ryan, he had overcompensated massively, knowing what was to come.

I took my little baby girl upstairs to her room and, in what was undoubtedly going to be one of the hardest experiences of my life, braced myself to tell her that her daddy was dead.

She loved him so much, even though it had been a year, she still spoke about him. She still idolised him, we still had his pictures up in the house.

I sat her down on the bed, surrounded by her toys.

"DJ, you know that your daddy loves you so, so much, don't you?" I asked, as she nodded her little head. "And you know that Daddy always wanted to see you, but it was Mummy's decision to not let him. You know that right?"

She was playing with her teddy, but looking at me, waiting for me to get to the point.

"He always loved you and always wanted to see you. But Mummy had to make sure that Daddy was well enough to look after you, because he was quite poorly. And Mummy could only let Daddy see you if he was well enough to."

She looked bemused but carried on looking up at me, while cuddling the teddy.

I sighed. Now or never.

"Sweetheart, Daddy went to heaven today. He died. Do you understand what I'm saying?"

She nodded. "Yes, Mummy," she said, and then just like that she picked up a different doll, and went back to playing with her toys.

She never really reacted. And to this day I worry that she kept it all bottled up then, and still does now. Was that a normal reaction for a child? I have no frame of reference.

She has so many little memories of her dad, but knowing she was never going to see him again was something that obviously affected me more than her at that point.

And how could it not? Molly and Lilly still have Brian, and while Heidi and Max don't have anything to do with Mark, at least there's an option there to reconnect with him one day, because he's still alive.

But little DJ has lost her daddy forever. And no matter what hell he put me through, he was still her father.

The guilt was palpable in that moment. If he had been allowed in DJ's life in that final year, would he still be alive today? But then would DJ? Would I?! He was too erratic and too ill and way too unpredictable. That's why I have to rise above the guilt and know I did the right thing for my child.

There was no way he could have had access to her while on so many drugs. He couldn't get himself clean for anyone. Not even DJ.

I wanted to stay with the kids that evening, but I knew the next day I had to face things. Regardless of the fact I hadn't seen George for well over a year, I was still his wife, and it was important for me to go to the Chapel of Rest and see his body. I needed to see him one last time. I was so angry at him for just dying on us after everything he'd put us through, I wanted to look at him and let him know. There would be no closure for me without that, at least.

Molly and I jumped in the car the day after George died, at 6am in the morning. It was going to be a long journey up north and emotionally I wasn't anywhere near ready to deal with it, so I figured if we went first thing we wouldn't have time to change our mind.

I shouldn't have worried, George was going to do his best to stop us getting up there from beyond the grave!

We were on the M25, driving along in the pissing rain, when suddenly the hands of the clock on the dashboard started going backwards, really fast. Then lights started flashing inside the car. The whole car immediately seemed impossible to control and we started swerving all over the show. I pulled over straight away and realised that out of nowhere, and for no logical reason I could fathom, our perfectly good car had just stopped working.

Someone didn't want us going to the Chapel of Rest.

Recovery came out and took us to a hire shop nearby to get another car. Only guess what? George was the one who last hired a car from them, under my account, and for a variety of reasons, probably including the fact he never actually gave the car back, I was banned from renting another vehicle.

This journey was not going well.

I called Ryan out, who came with DJ and hired a car under his name, while I hid in the car park. He returned with the keys and put them in my hand. I wasn't insured, granted, but getting to George was a bigger priority.

Lilly was still acting out at home, so I made the decision to send Molly back with Ryan. It made sense for her to be at home with the kids, rather than me.

I could sense little DJ wanted me and I was still so worried after her reaction the day before, I thought it was best that she stayed with me. So in effect I swapped my eldest for my youngest, and DJ came with me in the hire car for the rest of the journey.

Even now I have proper separation anxiety with DJ. I still need her with me when we're sleeping. I nearly had a breakdown a year after George's death, convincing myself he was coming back from the dead to give her cancer. I used to think, if God gave me George back for one day and I had the choice to give him DJ for that one day, I'd still say no. Knowing

# The End

George he'd take her with him. Finding out he wanted to inject her with heroin changed everything for me. It messed up my head beyond anything I've ever known and I know that fear has shaped my relationship with her. I'm so protective of that little girl and the thought of what he could've done to her leaves me with terrible anxiety, even now.

I hated being away from her and so at that point I needed her with me. That said, I drew the line at bringing her to the Chapel of Rest.

Instead, by the time we got up north, I took her straight to my mum's house, where I knew our friend Dawn would be able to watch her. I'd take Mum with me to the chapel.

Walking in there was the most surreal experience. The second I saw George's body I just collapsed on the floor, screaming.

I was sat on the ground, rocking back and forth, clutching my knees like a small child. The conflicting feelings overwhelmed my brain. I was so, so confused. So angry. The tears wouldn't stop falling.

"You dickhead!" I yelled. "How could you do this to us?! How could you put us through so much hell just to go and bloody die?!"

The people at the chapel must have wondered who on earth this complete loon was, but I couldn't stop myself. He was laying there, smirking, with dried blood all over his nose.

"You've left this beautiful little girl without a father! What have you done, you absolute dickhead?!"

In that moment I was so, so angry at him. How dare he put me through hell and just die like that?

We all knew it was inevitable, he was never going to change, but how dare he put me and the children through that amount of fear and anxiety, only to drop dead with no explanation? What was it all for?

At this point his body was no longer warm, he was deteriorating. Mum wanted me to give him a kiss, I think she believed it would help diffuse the intense anger and hysteria, but I just couldn't bring myself to do it. He didn't deserve it.

I took one last look at him. This cold, dead corpse. And, as if in a scene from a film, I could suddenly visualise him alive again. I could smell him, I could hear his voice, I could feel his soft skin. I could see him bent over the kitchen sink with a knife. I could see his clothes in the wardrobe, I could hear us laughing our heads off together as we cuddled in bed, I could see his fists as they came hurtling towards my face.

It was as if our entire relationship flashed before my eyes.

I shuddered and shook it off, pausing only one last time to sadly whisper, "Why, George? Why did you do it?" I wasn't sure if I was referring to the violence, the death, the drugs or all of it. All I knew is I'd never find out the answer.

Then, after being in that room for over an hour, battling feelings I never knew I had, I kissed him after all.

Although I can't express how angry I was in that moment, he was also my everything. He knew me better than anyone. I had so many conflicting feelings, I was struggling to hold it all together. I turned to leave. I would never, ever see George Kay, my husband, my tormentor, the great love of my life, ever again.

*****

I didn't go to the funeral, though I heard about it. I was invited, I just didn't want to go.

# The End

Even though George was lying in a coffin, I was still so scared of him. It took every ounce of strength in me to make it to the chapel, I just couldn't face the fear of going to the funeral. I felt like I didn't have the right to be there after everything. I felt like a hypocrite. I'd said my goodbyes in the Chapel of Rest, privately, and that's the way I wanted it to stay.

I know they played George Ezra's song Shotgun, which contains the lyrics 'See you later, gotta hit the road / There's a mountaintop that I'm dreaming of / If you need me you know where I'll be', which are pretty poignant.

I didn't want to be there and make it all about me. I didn't want it to become some sort of grotesque press circus. I heard George's brother started a Go Fund Me page to pay for it, which only inflamed the reports that George had died penniless.

I don't think for a second he was as broke as he was made out to be, though. In the year since he'd been off the scene, he'd been to Australia, Mexico, and he was also doing a course in fillers. He wanted to train in Botox! Can you imagine someone like George coming at your face with a needle?! And, really, how can an addict who was doing cocaine off a hotel bathroom sink be skint?

I did offer to help pay for the funeral, even though I had very little money at that point. But I felt, as his wife and DJ's mum, I should've done something. Even if it was a weekly direct debit. But I never heard back from his family about my offer. I didn't even know whether or not to send flowers on the day, so in the end I had nothing to do with it.

Instead I tried to distract myself and the kids by going to the cinema on the day George was cremated. We went to see the Lion King. I remember Brian McFadden putting some money into my bank so I could take them out. Molly was home from Ireland and I guess it was his way of contributing during that hard time. He was actually one of the first people to message me when George's death was announced. Regardless of our chequered past, he was there for me in that moment and that's something I won't forget.

It was my choice not to attend the funeral and the guilt remained. But I stick by my decision. I hadn't let George see DJ. I'd spoken publicly about what he'd done to me. I'd had a bloody restraining order taken out against him! I would've felt like such a hypocrite being there.

I guess in hindsight it was inevitable George was going to die and so for me, I'm glad it happened when DJ was young. So she never had to grow up witnessing the violence.

Of course the papers misconstrued my feelings on that front and the headlines splashed with 'Kerry: I'm glad George is dead!"

But that wasn't what I meant at all. And I was upset by that because I'd never want DJ to read that and think I wanted her daddy dead. I didn't.

I just meant I knew it would happen one day. And for the sake of our daughter I was glad it was sooner rather than later. Either way, it was inevitable.

His death left a huge hole in our lives, mainly because since the moment I fell in love with him, George had been all consuming. The drama, the abuse, the good times, the break-ups – everything revolved around our relationship. Even in death he'd managed to make it all about him because now I was a shell.

Completely devastated.

## The End

I was angry at George, I was sad for my children. I felt guilty over the fact Ryan was having to watch me mourn my husband and I was conflicted by George's parents' reaction to it all. They seemed to hate me.

And when the inquest into his death began, I realised just how much.

# 11

# The Truth Will Out

It was two years after George's death when the inquest took place at Warrington Coroner's Court. In that time I'd moved on with Ryan, we were building our future and life had managed to miraculously get itself back on course, which I'll go into later.

I had been feeling happy and optimistic, but the inquest itself really threw me. In fact it set me back. I was drained emotionally and I was hurt I wasn't even invited to attend. I was still George's wife at the end of the day – the man never divorced me. Don't get me wrong, I wouldn't have gone out of respect, but I felt like I at least should have been invited so I could get answers for my daughter. Why should I find out from the papers how my child's dad died? Why did I not deserve to be given the information in person like the rest of his family? I was the mother of his only child, and she would be asking questions as she got older about how her daddy died. How could they not think of DJ?!

I found the whole situation incredibly hard. But then I should've known what to expect.

In those two years since his funeral, I didn't hear anything from George's mum and dad. I really believed it was in DJ's best interests to have a relationship with her grandparents, but they wouldn't even respond to my messages asking them to video call with her, which killed me. DJ absolutely idolised her granddad and would often talk about her cousins.

I don't know whether their change of heart had anything to do with their grief over George, or because of the hell George had put them through as a family, or indeed if it was their own issues. But it wasn't DJ's fault and I believe she should have been acknowledged.

I did go and see them as soon as George died. His dad told me that George tried to set the house on fire and had hidden in a wardrobe thinking monsters were coming to get him in the week before he passed.

It made me realise just how much he'd put them through as well, but the idea they'd snub DJ completely once George went – it was bizarre to me.

They were never, ever stopped from seeing her.

I went round to theirs just before we went to the Chapel of Rest. His dad looked like the weight of the world was suddenly off his shoulders. He and George's mum spoke about how many times he'd been hospitalised. His brother was there too, reminiscing and telling me how he was sure George would never grow old. They also knew George would never have taken his own life, which is what the inquest was due to determine.

Once I'd gone back down south I would send them videos and pictures of DJ, dancing or learning to ride her bike. I asked how the funeral went and they told me it went well. I then asked if DJ could have some of her dad's ashes – but I never heard from them again.

To this day I don't understand what happened with the communication breakdown, or why they said such shocking things about me at the inquest. I get that I'd spoken out about George in the past, we obviously had an incredibly volatile relationship and yes, there had been a restraining order in place before he died. But there was a reason I'd addressed it all publicly. I was a celebrity, and his family knew full well I couldn't lay low with all the shit George had put me through. The press would be reporting on it regardless.

And they knew what he was like! They knew how troubled and mentally ill he was and they knew he was heavily into drugs.

What was I supposed to do? I couldn't keep my daughter around him while he was so poorly and they had to understand that as well.

In 2020, I got a message out of the blue from somebody close to the family, telling me George's dad was in a bad way. Of course this was upsetting enough, I'd always liked George's dad and the thought of him being ill was horrible.

But what followed in the message was a big shock.

"If you have any morals about you, you'll let him see DJ", the message spat.

I stared at my screen trying to take in the words. Was this person being serious? They want me to take a seven-year-old to see a dying man who'd refused to see her for two years?! And they're questioning MY morals? That's the first time anybody had texted me about DJ since George passed. And even more ridiculous, it was the first time this person had ever actually messaged me – about anything! They'd never once asked after DJ, or even sent her a birthday card.

The anger rose inside of me. It felt completely unjust being spoken to in this way. I had been fighting to get them to see DJ for so long, and now George's dad was dying they decided it was appropriate? The little girl had been through so, so much over the course of that time, I wasn't going to subject her to it. I'd spent too much time making excuses to DJ.

"I'm sorry he's unwell but I'm not doing it," I replied. "It's going to mess DJ's head up."

I was not going to subject her to go and see a dying man like that. She hadn't heard from her nan and granddad in two years, not even a birthday card or a FaceTime, and so many times she'd asked about them. I just didn't think it was fair on her. This was not about me being cruel, this was about what was best for DJ.

I spent a long time debating whether or not I was doing the right thing. It took a lot of soul searching and I do wonder if my decision that day drove them to say such awful things about me at the inquest. Maybe if I'd played ball they wouldn't have done it. Either way, what they said about me wasn't true, and now is my chance to tell people that.

It was August 2021 and the family had gathered to find out exactly what happened in George's last hours.

It involved statements from his family, and as far as I'm concerned they wasted no time in placing the blame on me – despite the fact I'd not seen him in the 18 months before he died.

His brother told the court that George's drug intake had gotten worse when he was with me. I agree in a way, George's drug intake was more obvious in the latter years we were together, but it certainly wasn't worse. The guy had been in prison for six years, he was an addict for God's sake. He always had problems. I wasn't touching the stuff, so there was no way they could've said I was encouraging the drug abuse. I would see the way it made him. The paranoia, the fear – I was the one begging him to stop.

But still he stuck by his statement.

"We want to make clear that the drug taking period increased during his time with his wife and got significantly worse when they separated, due to the fact he was stopped from seeing his child," he said.

Talk about laying the blame at my door. As I pointed out a million times, he was stopped from seeing his daughter because he refused to get help and he was becoming a danger to her and himself.

His mum also made out like I'd introduced George to drugs. The same woman who warned me before my wedding not to go through with it due to the fact he was an addict. How could she possibly even believe what she was saying?

I understand their desire to defend George in death, but the truth is the truth.

Her statement was in a similar vein to his brother's.

She said, "George was a lovely lad. He made friends easily, he was kind and he would do anything to help anyone." She added, "There were personal difficulties he had in his life that may have led to him taking more recreational drugs. He had a social life at that time which revolved around celebrity friends that would provide him with money and there was talk about helping him set up a business abroad."

What they were saying blew my mind. How could they blame his drug use on our 'personal difficulties'? There was so, so much more to George's mental health issues than just our marriage. Yes, we had huge problems and no I won't apologise for stopping him from seeing DJ. But in George's mind, things went far deeper than that. And as for these 'celebrity friends'? I'm pretty sure most dropped off radar once we split for good.

It all felt like such a big kick in the teeth.

*****

George's dad passed away, sadly, and it's something I feel upset about for DJ's sake. Maybe one day, on her own terms and not on his, she could have found a way to reconnect with her granddad. I don't have any contact with his mum or brother now and that suits me. But if they ever wanted to see DJ, the door is open. I just need to make sure it's in my child's best interests, as that's the most important thing to me.

The inquest wasn't just an excuse for George's family to blame me for his death. It was also a chance to discover exactly what happened that day in the Holiday Inn.

We found out he'd been hallucinating and that an unnamed female police officer had later been disciplined for not arresting him there and then, despite an estimated £100 worth of high purity cocaine being found in George's bathroom.

She told the court, "It looked like he had sniffed a line of cocaine off the side of the sink. If there was half a teaspoon of cocaine, I would have taken it as analysis but there wasn't much there at all. I did not believe it was enough to arrest him for possession of drugs. The remnants of cocaine were left in the bathroom. I was mainly concerned about his welfare."

More police officers and hotel workers stepped forward to give evidence as well, divulging details of George's behaviour the night before he died.

One officer said: "The hotel staff were concerned about a male wandering around and banging on doors refusing to go back to his room. When we got there, he was quite calm. We understand that he had been taking drugs. He said he had taken the substance in the bathroom about one hour before. He said he had been seeing shadows and that he saw wasps in his room. We realised he had been hallucinating. He said he was struggling with his mental health because of issues in his personal life. He admitted to taking cocaine that evening."

As I read all this, it was becoming clear to me that George had simply taken too many drugs. Any notion this was suicide or foul play just wasn't correct. No chance. It sounded more sad than anything else.

A lady called Caroline Garcia, who worked at the hotel reiterated the point.

"At around 7pm a colleague rang me to say there was a guest in the corridor making noise," she said. "I went to see what was going on and there was a strong, tall man speaking with another lady outside one of the rooms. I thought he was drunk or high and I dealt with the situation. He was not making any sense and said he was looking for someone to be his friend."

This detail is something that makes me tearful to this day. George, as he so often became when he was on drugs, was clearly scared, lonely and desperate. The description of him reminded me of the video when he was up on the roof, naked and yelling. That same vulnerability and childishness, locked up in a big, strong body.

This Caroline was obviously a prominent figure in the last hours of George's life, as she apparently helped him when he was particularly confused. She had asked for his ID to help him find his hotel room, but he didn't play ball. She'd managed to get him into a lift and stayed with him for an hour, while other hotel workers tried to get him to drink water, which he couldn't seem to swallow.

She then went on to reveal, "(George) asked if I would prepare cocaine for him, but I said I wouldn't do that. He said there was a man in his room but we went to his room and we confirmed there was no one else there. He was refusing to go into the room and was saying it was not his."

Other staff said that George had been behaving "erratically" and "unpredictably" but no one apparently thought he was a threat. Maybe he wasn't to anyone else, but he sure was to himself.

Whatever the case, George appeared to make it back into his room that night, but the next morning, bizarrely, he needed help from housekeeping to let him back in. I don't think anyone really knows what went on in those lost few hours or why he'd managed to lock himself out. Did he venture out? Did he sleep somewhere else? Did he stay up doing more drugs? Whatever the case, clearly he hadn't sobered up by the time the sun rose.

Another hotel worker gave the following account of what happened in the morning George died, having eventually helped him back into the room.

"He pulled out a sock with a large ball and was sat in a chair," the inquest was told. "He caused the ball to crumble by crushing it and I believed it was drugs. He became very unwell, so we put him in the recovery position and called an ambulance."

As we all know, George died later, having eaten those drugs, and snorted God knows how much more of the stuff the previous night.

As the details came to light, it really did shock me more than I thought possible. I knew it was a tragic way to die, but the loneliness he must have felt, the helplessness and the fear he would've experienced as he hallucinated – I can't bear the thought of it.

This is the man who put me through hell, yet in spite of it all, I still cry when I think about the way he died.

His death was officially ruled as 'drug related', which was a relief in some ways, considering some people with practically zero knowledge of the situation had tried to imply it was suicide.

The assistant coroner gave the following verdict: "*Police officers were called to attend because Mr Kay was behaving in an effective manner. He admitted to taking drugs, he was calm and police did not consider it lawful to arrest or search him. They did not think he required an urgent medical assessment and they left. On the morning of 6 July, he was seen to eat a quantity of cocaine and then collapse. It is not possible to say how he came into possession of the cocaine he took on that morning but I am satisfied the death was drug related.*"

And just like that, George's story was over.

His entire demise summarised in a few short sentences, before the court moved on to another case. It all felt like such a terrible waste. Everything we'd been through together, the ups and downs, the happiness, the violence, our every experience, what was it all for? He put me through hell, only to go ahead and drop dead after eating coke from a sock.

The only comfort I get is knowing our marriage brought us DJ. I'd do it all again, ten times over, if it means having my little girl. She was a blessing in a very dark time.

# The Truth Will Out

Sometimes I'll sit down, as I've done to write this book, and think of the good times with George. And there really were so many. But the shadow of violence and fear always loomed large over us.

I wish he'd been wired differently. I wish he hadn't been so cruel. I wish he was charming and funny and lovable the entire time we were together, like I knew he could be.

But you can't change the past – and you can't change the man.

And more than anything, I can't bring him back.

Maybe it's for the best. Life after George was tough in places but I found a renewed strength. I swore after he died, I would never, ever allow myself to be put through that again.

Everything I owned, I was taking responsibility for. I was going to make my money back. I was going to get my career back. I was going to embrace love with Ryan, a wonderful man who made me feel safe, a feeling which up until that point had been largely alien to me. I was going to love *myself* and more than any of that – I was going to be the best mum I could possibly be.

I was going to come back fighting.

# 12

# Staying Strong

In the months that followed George's death, life slowly returned to some sort of normality – a different sort, I suppose, following the shockwave that had reverberated through all our lives.

Having seen first hand what an amazing rock Ryan had been through it all, I was well and truly invested in our love by this point. I could see a future with him and, even though I was still wary of marriage and more kids, I felt confident that that would be our end game regardless. Never before had a man treated me with such respect and kindness and to this day, I could never thank him enough for the way he handled it all.

Still, despite my increasing contentment with Ryan, it was impossible to shake the trauma of what we'd been through and I noticed a steady decline in my mental health as a result.

It's hard to explain, but as someone who famously suffers from bipolar, it's not something you can just 'snap out of'. I spent many days in bed battling with my feelings. I was still grieving George, and with that came an enormous sense of guilt. Guilt for the children and what they were going through, and guilt due to the fact I was with Ryan and it felt strange to be grieving the death of my husband while another man lay in my bed.

I was especially struggling with the kids, who were dealing with the loss in their own way. I was particularly worried about DJ, but in hindsight she was the one who probably coped the best. I know Heidi had a tough time and Max was playing up too, so all this was weighing heavily on me as I tried to figure out how to combat it.

I spent a lot of time in those days looking back at the way I'd been treated by the public and the media when it came to my mental health and wondering how it was ever acceptable.

I still look back on my infamous 'This Morning' interview in 2008 with mixed feelings. I'm not ashamed of it, because I have nothing to be ashamed of. And I'm pleased people can see it now and know the truth. But I'm sad I was ever put through the ridicule that followed. Treatment like that wouldn't be acceptable now.

For anyone reading this who may not know (I'll assume you've been living under a rock, as it's up there with my most 'infamous' moments), I went on live TV, being interviewed by Phillip Schofield and Fern Britton, slurring my words due to the fact I was on my bipolar medication. The next day the headlines screamed, "Kerry's Car Crash interview!" and "Sherry Kerry", the implication of course being that I was off my face on drink and drugs.

Well, as I've pointed out time and time again, I wasn't. But it took me years to come back from that. The sheer cruelty of the public after that left me suicidal. Thank God social media wasn't a big thing at the time, or I'm not sure I'd have come through it. It was bad enough just seeing the response in the press.

Thankfully, although sites like Twitter and Instagram are still cesspits for trolls with too many opinions, the world is changing rapidly and people are a lot more tolerant and accepting of mental health struggles. And it couldn't come soon enough.

During those This Morning times, my doctor told me not to tell anyone I had bipolar. Mental illness was too taboo. Of course hypothetically I could shout it from the rooftops about having a drink and drug problem, but bipolar? "You'd better keep that under your hat, Kerry. People won't understand it," they said. "If people can't see something, they won't get it."

I got diagnosed in 2005 with my illness and the This Morning interview was in 2008. When I went to rehab during that time people just assumed I was in The Priory for drink and drug issues. I wasn't. I was in there to deal with my bipolar, doing trial and error with my medication to make sure the dosage was right. At one point I was dribbling non-stop like a baby. They couldn't seem to find the right meds and it did leave me virtually incapacitated. It was never booze, never drugs. It was my illness and I was absolutely slaughtered publicly for it by people who didn't have the slightest clue what I was going through. Even after going public with the illness, people would cross the road to avoid me. They didn't have any idea. Even Brian McFadden didn't know what it was – he thought bipolar was a bloody sport!

It was only when Catherine Zeta Jones, Hollywood royalty, spoke about it, that everyone started to take it more seriously. In this industry you have to be a certain calibre to be listened to.

Look at Ant McPartlin, he's had his demons and they've been well documented. He crashed a car after drinking alcohol and took time out to attend rehab. But he had so much sympathy in a way I didn't and was back on TV within a few months. I really believe that was because he is a prime time star, no kids of his own, and he's a man. Just for the record I'm just using Ant as an example – I absolutely adore him and applaud him on his sobriety, but I'm trying to make a point as to how women are treated differently to men, especially when you're from a working class background like myself.

Look then at all these rock stars, many who are fathers, and who talk about all the orgies and drugs they've done in their time. It's all lapped up by the media and the public and they're considered heroes! But put me on TV, slurring my words because of the medication I'm on to treat a verified medical disorder and people are calling for social services to get involved. The double standards were horrifying. One rule for one and all that.

The reason I bring it up now is because I find the changing attitudes toward mental illness so interesting. I had to fight so bloody hard to come back from that time in my life, to convince people I wasn't some junkie. It was hell and in hindsight it was so utterly unnecessary.

I know having been open and honest about my issues, that people would be a lot more supportive of me if I ended up back in rehab now. I speak so openly and honestly about my fears and anxiety, that people have had to sit up and pay attention. But we're still not quite there. We have been educated a lot about mental health and I like to think I'm playing a big part in that. I'm such an advocate for it and it's something I believe we still need to talk about more.

Because I'm a woman, I've been married multiple times, I've got kids with different men – why's it my fault? Yes I have five children by three fathers, but I'm the one raising them! Where's the vitriol for the men who plant their seed and bugger off?!

Look at Boris Johnson. He's got all these different kids with different women and he's got Prime Minister on his CV!

Sometimes it feels like I'm being judged totally unfairly and it angers me. I'm the one who puts the kids to bed every night, I work to make sure they have everything, and I'm the one who doesn't complain because I love them so much. So why does everyone else care? Does anyone have a go at Brian, a world-famous pop star who's daddy to my daughters? The sheer double standards really winds me up and it's no wonder women like me suffer mentally as a result.

I really believe it's because I'm from a council estate as well. Ulrika Johnson, she has children with different men and I think she's treated differently from me too. But you only have to meet my children or see them on the TV and you can see how well behaved, polite and kind they are. I've done everything in my power to make sure they don't have the same upbringing as me. I had to work hard and I've always been a grafter. My kids now have private education because that's something I can provide.

I took Max out the other day for dinner at a nice restaurant and he had olives and prawns, and the way he eloquently ordered this food, for a young lad, was so impressive. I've made sure we're now well educated and well travelled enough that all my lot can appreciate different foods. And they do. Pâté, mussels, lobster – they love it all. I couldn't even read a menu when I was that age. I thought chicken fajitas was a chicken foetus until I was 18. I once went to a Chinese restaurant with my high school boyfriend and his parents and thought the finger bowl they gave us was soup. I'd never been to a Chinese before. I just didn't know. My local restaurant was a chippy!

Even in Atomic Kitten, I'd have to get my manager to read

the menu when I was with the girls so I didn't look like an idiot when I was ordering. I wasn't educated. I'm actually smart and intelligent, I'm super clued-up and great with business and I'm streetwise too, but I'm just no good academically. Maths, spelling, anything like that is not my forte.

I can say now that people do seem to be on my side again. I was nicknamed the nation's sweetheart when I won my series of I'm A Celebrity, but I soon messed that up and was swiftly replaced by Cheryl Cole. Did you know at one point the media – I can't remember which publication specifically – did a poll and I was voted runner-up in the Most Hated Person in Britain 'award'? Camilla Parker Bowles was first and I was second. I went from being the nation's sweetheart to being detested overnight. All because I fell for the wrong man. I met Mark Croft and subsequently I experienced the biggest fall from grace, all at my own hands of course – I take responsibility – but how crazy to think during that time I was allowed to be treated like that, just because I made bad choices for myself. I was nicknamed the British Britney Spears!

But I do think now, thanks to my awareness of mental health, people are beginning to see the real me again. Finally. After all this time.

*****

When I look back on the young women who were subjected to so much while in the spotlight, the likes of Sarah Harding, Jade Goody and Caroline Flack, it breaks my heart they're no longer with us.

Caroline reached out to me just before she died in February

2020, as she'd been targeted by the Fathers 4 Justice group, just as I had been after George's death. Caroline had been arrested for supposedly attacking her boyfriend in the night with a lamp and was due to stand trial but took her own life before that happened. By all accounts F4J were on her case, despite the fact it had nothing whatsoever to do with any children or custody battles.

I'd contacted her on Instagram in the December, just to show support after ITV unfairly dropped her from her presenting gig on Love Island as a result of the charges. She replied saying, 'Thanks Kerry, that means so much.'

A couple of weeks later she messaged me again. 'How did you deal with Fathers 4 Justice?' she asked. 'They're horrible.'

I honestly felt my blood boil straight away. Knowing what they'd put me through and now they were targeting Caroline during what would've been one of the toughest periods of her life, just made me rage.

'Don't tell me they're on your case?!' I wrote back, seething. 'Honestly babe, I thought I was going to have a nervous breakdown! They accused me of killing my husband! It was awful! But these people are just trying to make headlines… at the end of the day I know the truth! And I had to reassure myself that other people's opinions of me mean nothing!! You've got this darling! Don't let the fuckers bring you down. Show them how strong you are!!! xxx'

She responded immediately. Even over message, I could feel the pain in her words. 'How do they get away with it?' she begged. 'It's bullying and making me sink so deep.'

My heart broke for her. I had been exactly where she was just a few months before.

# Staying Strong

'Honestly, I feel your pain,' I wrote back. 'It made me so ill, but I promise you, you will get through this!. I was going to take legal action but I just didn't want to give them the press attention.'

Caroline replied in such a sweet way, thinking of me rather than herself.

'I can't imagine what you've been through', she wrote. 'I'm so sorry. x'

I felt so protective of her in those moments, knowing exactly what she was dealing with. I responded with a rallying cry, urging her to stay strong. 'Come on, you've got this. Don't let them win.'

She replied, 'Means a lot and I won't forget it.'

I didn't hear from her again.

She took her own life just eight weeks later.

Like the rest of the country, her death really hit me hard. To me, Caroline was as big a star as Ant and Dec or Dermot O'Leary. She was in a different bracket of celebrity to me, I was much more a reality/pop star, whereas she was a bonafide, talented prime time TV presenter. And she exuded class. I thought she was amazing.

I saw the documentary her mum and sister made about a year after her death, in which it was clear Caroline would obsessively check social media to see what the trolls were saying about her and I get that. I do it too, even now. It's so hard not to. As I've said already, I was suicidal when George died. And at the same time I was being blamed for his death. Caroline must have felt the terrible weight of judgement over what happened with her and her fella. The pressure she must have been under. Her story and her fate could easily have been so, so different. And that's what hit me harder than anything when she died. I know if I didn't have my children I wouldn't be here right now, telling this story.

I wish I could've done more to help her, but there is some comfort in knowing my messages bought her some solace around that time. If only she'd have held on a bit longer, when Covid took over the whole world, she might have got through it. We'll never know.

*****

It's become a real ambition of mine now to travel the country teaching people about mental health and how we should be tackling it. It's no longer a taboo subject but it's one I have more authority than most to talk about. My own struggles, watching George's decline, it's all been part of my story and I know I have the tools to help other people.

I'm so sick of being considered a 'warning' case, I'm actually a prime example of someone who's survived, against all odds.

I think growing up the way I did, on a council estate, surrounded by abusive men, I was always going to have issues. There's no way you can sit back and see the things I saw and not be affected. And the fact I genuinely suffer from bipolar, which impacts my life on a day to day basis, is another hurdle. But as I write this book, I realise just how far I've come. I never, ever gave up and I still fight every day to make sure people see the real me.

It's no surprise that women like Caroline die by suicide. The pressure on them to be perfect all the time, to make the right decisions, to fight back against keyboard warriors with nothing better to do than spit vitriol from behind their laptops, it's too much for anyone, let alone someone in the public eye.

Watching Lilly's star rise as she does more and more TV shows with me now, I'm conscious I don't want her looking at too much social media or reviews, as I don't want her opinion of herself to be dictated by other people.

But hopefully the tide is turning in the #BeKind era.

Of course it's not just Joe Public or the media who can influence the state of your mental health. As I found with George, a lot of stresses and strains come from within the family itself. And, as I say, growing up the way I did I know that a lot of my demons stem from childhood.

I've had such a tricky relationship with my mum, Sue, as a result of it, much of which I've written down in my last two books.

But as my children get older – and as *I* get older – it's interesting to see how key that mother and daughter bond truly is to someone's mental health and it's something I've been thinking a lot about over the last few years.

Surviving George, both the abuse and his death, is something I watched Mum do with her own partner too. It's weird how history repeats itself, though there's no question my mum's own struggles as a result of what she went through have almost destroyed her. I know full well it's almost destroyed our relationship on many occasions, and even now things can be tense between us.

I've always been aware that I don't want to end up like her.

I'm not trying to be cruel, or rude, it's just a fact of life.

She's a difficult woman and she's lived a hard life and now she's paying the price for her mistakes.

## Kerry Katona

She doesn't seem to have the strength to overcome what she's been through and it's something that makes me so sad.

More than anything, I wish she'd try just a little bit harder.

# 13

## Family Ties

So as I've said, it's no secret me and my mum Sue have had a complicated relationship since day one. I've spoken and written about it countless times before, because to me, it's one of – if not *the* most – significant and challenging relationships in my life.

We've been through so much. We've done drugs together. I ended up in foster homes as a teenager because she couldn't take care of me. We've been estranged for years after she sold a story on me to the tabloids. I've watched as she's tried to take her own life on multiple occasions.

But despite the many hardships, she's still my mum. She's still the person I want when I'm feeling ill. She's still the one who knows me better than anyone.

Ryan and I decided to make the move back up north during the latter days of the Covid crisis in 2021. I was so devastated by the loss of my Aunty Angela, which I'll go into later, that a change seemed like a good idea. To be nearer Mum, to be nearer home. Plus I wanted to get away from the memories of George in Crowborough.

I was so excited to be back with her, starting a new chapter with Ryan and the kids and having her close by.

But the problem with Mum is her lifestyle choices, namely her drinking.

It was May 2022 and I got the call I was dreading. With Mum it was never a case of 'if' she'd have a heart attack – it was 'when'.

I was getting my tattoo done when our friend Dawn rang me.

"I don't want you to panic, but your mum's had a heart attack," she said.

Surprisingly I was dead calm. So calm in fact I carried on getting my tatt done!

The ambulance people said we weren't allowed to see her thanks to Covid. But at this point I wasn't overly worried because I knew she was ok. Plus Dawn said she'd keep me up to date with any news from the hospital.

There was nothing I could do, and to be honest I was annoyed with Mum because we all saw this coming a mile off.

I think the kids were more freaked out by the fact I was so chilled about me mum being in hospital than the heart attack itself! But like I said, I knew it was coming. It's another reason we made the move up north. For when something like this inevitably happened to her.

I had my commitments with panto at that point so I couldn't be with her straight away anyway, but I needn't have worried. When I did make it down to the hospital she looked like she was in her bloody element! Top dog on the ward, weren't she?! Barking out orders, telling jokes. It was the best I'd seen her look in a long while. Now *this* was the mum I adore!

She hadn't drunk alcohol in days and she was in great form.

It was proof, if needed, that she just doesn't get out enough. She's got herself in such a rut, she sits in that bloody flat day after day, drinking by herself. She's missing out on so much life! Seeing her in that hospital, surrounded by people and just being anywhere but her sofa, it had made such a difference.

When it comes to me mum, I wish she'd try a little bit more with her health. She has five gorgeous grandkids who want her to stick around, so why doesn't she get herself healthier? She's quit the fags, which is brilliant, but she's holding on to that booze. It breaks my heart because I know how much she loves those children. But she's powerless when it comes to the drink. I managed to reset my brain and change my mindset – in fact she's the reason I quit smoking, I couldn't bear to hear her cough up that phlegm and I didn't want to be like that – and I get frustrated that she can't do the same.

This isn't me slagging her off, this is me worried about her, angry and wishing she could be the best version of herself she could be. It's annoying from my point of view more than anything because I know she could change things up a bit. Maybe it's frustration on my part. Or maybe it's just me missing my mum. Either way I desperately want her to stick around for a lot longer!

I have so many health problems with my back, hip and shoulders and I suffer from chronic pain as a result. But when I complain about the pain it reminds me so much of my mum. And I so, so don't want to be like her. Believe me, I'm trying everything – painkillers, yoga, exercise – I don't want to be eighty when I'm sixty!

Mum is who she is. When I lived down south I used to get so upset, wishing she was closer to me, physically. I would've done anything in those moments to just snap my fingers and be at her side in an instant.

But now, being up here again, it's different somehow. The reality has hit home. The illusion is crushed. I always thought she'd be round loads, she'd be babysitting, we'd spend the days together, but it hasn't happened like that. She barely leaves her flat.

*****

One day, not long before she ended up in hospital, she suffered a mild angina attack.

"Did you ring the doctor's, Mum?" I asked when she called me to tell me.

"No, I don't want to go to the doctors!"

Sigh. Now, if that was me and I'd just had an angina attack, I'd be looking at every which way I could to change my lifestyle.

"Mum, please when that happens you have to call the doctor!"

By this point I was so fed up, I was past the point of being scared about the angina attack. I just went off on one.

"One day you're going to die, alone in your flat, and I'm going to be the one who finds you," I yelled down the phone. "I really thought when our Angela died, that would be the wake-up call you needed!"

Angela, her beloved baby sister, was just 51 years old when she died of alcoholism.

But nothing gets through to me mum. The bottom line is she's powerless to her addictions.

I no longer answer the phone to her after 5pm because I know she'll have had a drink. She's so blind to it she truly believes she's not drunk. As a family we only have to hear her say "hello" and we can tell she's pissed. She says she's not hurting anyone (apart from herself) which is true – but I just can't bear the false persona. We all love going round me mum's but as soon as that wine bottle comes out I see Molly and Lilly rolling their eyes.

But please be assured, I love her to bits. And this all comes from a place of love and fear over what could happen to her. I'll always have her back. After all, she's the only mum I have.

She has come on leaps and bounds from the person she was, but she's not quite there yet. For instance, our friend Dawn will call her up and ask her to come and watch DJ playing rounders, or see her in her school play. DJ would love to look out into the crowd and see her nanny-nue there, but it's so hard to get her out of that bloody flat and as a result she misses out on so much! It's heartbreaking.

That said, for all her faults, I'm also dead grateful to her, because growing up with her has made me so resilient. It's made me the person I am today. I'm now able to help others who have been in similar situations because I understand what it means to stand on your own.

What I should also point out is that she's there for me in the moments I'm at my lowest. Even when I was writing the most devastating parts of this book, I'd go and sit with her to recall the hard times. And boy did she step up when George died. She was amazing. As I said earlier, she came with me to the Chapel of Rest and held me while I sobbed. She was my rock at that point and I know exactly why. It was my marriage to George that she identified with most, because she'd been there.

Mine and George's relationship very much mirrors the romance she had with a man named Dave Wheat, a convicted murderer who's mentioned in my first book and is the reason I was put into a foster home. He stabbed my mum, screaming that he was Freddy Kreuger and said he was gonna, "Cut our tits and fanny off, chop us up and put us in the fridge".

We're not talking about a nice bloke here. He was inside with The Krays (we even got a Christmas card from Reggie) – that's the kind of guy we were dealing with. Dave would beat the hell out of her, but yet he was the love of her life.

As a kid, witnessing the beatings, I would think, 'You can go through that a million times, but once would be enough for me.' And yet I ended up doing exactly the same thing.

I told Mum years later, "I get it." These men groom you. It's so easy for people on the outside to say, "Why don't you just leave?" but it's not that simple.

Dave died when he was run over by a car, and that was when Mum really hit rock bottom.

One day, shortly after he was killed, when I was about 15, she sat there on a chair in the corner of her flat and told me, "That's it, I want to die. I want to be dead, I've got nothing here for me."

"What about me, Mum?" I asked as that familiar sense of dread started to rise in my stomach. "Are you really going to kill yourself and leave me here?"

But then, as if a switch had suddenly gone off in my head, my fear was replaced with anger.

"You know what? If that's how you feel, let's do it."

I went into the bathroom, grabbed a bottle of pills and told her to take them.

"Keep taking them! Eat them all," I urged as she did what she was told.

She swallowed the whole bottle.

"And now I'm going to ring you an ambulance, you selfish, selfish woman", I said. I dialled 999. I explained what had happened and then I turned back to my mum and said, "Right, I've got my GCSEs tomorrow. I've got to go back to my foster parents. The ambulance is on its way."

Of course she survived. And life just seemed to carry on as normal. In a strange mix of fear and worry and pure sadness.

Mum was so, so damaged by Dave and what he'd put us through, that she understood how I felt about George. I had so many mixed emotions about George's death and the way he'd treated me and she understood that. She went through exactly the same thing herself. Seriously, when I say she was my rock, I'm not lying.

So you won't be surprised to hear that she loved George at the start. Remember how I said he threw the phone at my head just weeks after we began dating? She didn't seem to see the huge red flag standing right in front of her.

She was totally blinded by him. She adored him. When I went to bootcamp he would go and stay at hers every night while I was away! She'd make him tea. It was only some time later when George turned on her and kicked her door down that she saw him for what he was worth. And when I fell pregnant with DJ, I remember her looking at me and saying "Oh God – you're stuck with him now."

Yet still, she understood. She'd been there.

Now, with both George and Dave long gone, I just want her to focus on being the best grandmother she can be. She's only 62. If she gets to her 80th, that'll be 18 Christmases she'll see with her family.

I would do anything to make her more sociable. I beg her:

"Try and do something with your days!" I know when I'm on my deathbed, I'll be able to hold my head high and say with complete certainty that I did the best I could in this life.

I wish more than anything my mum could say the same.

\*\*\*\*\*

Being a mum now I look at motherhood in a different way. I didn't feel that loved growing up, but that's life, I don't hold resentment towards Mum because of it. It's the cards we've been dealt. And trust me when I say me mum had a particularly shitty hand.

I never ever want my kids to feel unloved by their mum or unworthy. Ever. I've done a lot of daft things but those five children know how loved they are.

That said, I know I need to recognise that while my kids have never watched me slit my wrists, or swallow a bottle of pills, or seen me high on drugs, their trauma is just as significant to them as it was for me when I was young. All the moving, the awful husbands I've had, the bipolar – I can't belittle what they've been through thanks to me. But I own it.

And you know what? I don't harbour any hatred towards Mum for what we've been through. It made me who I am. I just know, as I write this, I'm in a place where I am stronger – WE are stronger – as a result of what we've experienced together. And it's made me all the more determined to make sure my own kids are never, ever short on love.

# 14

# Health Anxiety

We were in the midst of a pandemic and the outside world was falling apart. But in my life, things were going brilliantly, at last.

It was a year and a half since George's death and, although I know it's not something I'll be able to get over, life was moving on. Despite the awful situation Covid had put us all in, I was personally feeling on top of the world.

I was madly in love with Ryan, the kids were thriving, work was going well and I was making a good chunk of money for the first time in a long time.

But, as is often the case with me, the good times don't last long. There's always a spanner to be thrown into the works!

Out of the blue I'd received a private message from a fan, who was writing to tell me they'd seen a recent picture of me on a photoshoot, and they'd noticed a worrying-looking lump under my arm. Now, I know this sounds awful, but I initially ignored her. I wasn't interested in anything bursting my little bubble of happiness. Besides, when I'd shaved and washed before I hadn't seen or felt anything. Admittedly I understood what she meant when I saw the picture, but I put the slightly misshapen flesh down to my recent breast surgery.

It was then, one day in the shower, I was washing when I felt the lump under my arm. This wasn't long after the surgery, so there could've been any number of reasons for it. But of course, to me, as a woman approaching my forties, there was only one explanation.

Cancer.

My heart started to race. This wasn't good. I struggled to keep upright as my legs suddenly turned to jelly. Why had I not listened to that fan?! They had seen what I hadn't even been able to feel!

It felt like in a single moment, all my power was taken from me.

I can control whether or not I do drugs. I can control stopping smoking. I can control my weight, my finances, all that. But this was something completely different. I've turned my whole life around, and now this is it. I've got cancer. I'm going to die.

I collapsed onto the floor of the shower, sobbing while the water came flooding down on me. But the weight of the hot liquid was nothing compared to the sudden emotional weight on my shoulders. I can't leave my kids! I can't die! I haven't even got a will in place!

It was made worse by the obvious fear I saw in Ryan's eyes when I told him. He didn't say much, but you could see he was freaked out.

I knew I had to calm down and think rationally.

I'm ashamed to say now that even then, as scared as I was, I was even more scared of overwhelming the NHS at the height of the pandemic. But I knew I had no choice. I got myself straight down to my GP.

Luckily enough my doctor was amazing and I was able to get an appointment pretty quickly. And although Ryan came with me, I had to go in alone, such were the restrictions at the time. But the doctor was so hot on making sure any lump was seen to as a priority, for which I will be forever grateful for.

So, shortly after my 40th birthday, they sent me for a mammogram, scans and tests, something I had to face alone for obvious reasons at the time. I remember sitting in the waiting room, closing my eyes and genuinely seeing my life flash before me.

It's clichéd to say, but it really did happen like that.

Thoughts flooded my brain – 'What will happen to my kids? Will they get split up when I die? Will this affect them for the rest of their lives?'

The nurse came to get me. By this point I was crying and shaking so much she had to help me up, holding my arm like I was a frail old lady and leading me to a little room to take the tests.

I've been through so much in my life, often at the hand of other people. But this was different. This was mother nature, biology, God, calling the shots. I felt utterly powerless and I wept uncontrollably.

All this happened not long after Sarah Harding, the gorgeous Girls Aloud singer and someone I was privileged enough to know, had gone public about her breast cancer diagnosis. That hit me like a ton of bricks because it makes you realise we're not invincible. Your whole mortality is thrown into question. You have no control, it's all a matter of odds. It doesn't matter if you're a popstar, a lollipop lady, a lawyer or the queen of bloody England, cancer doesn't discriminate.

Thankfully, when the results came back for me it was good news. Something that couldn't be said for poor, sweet Sarah. Apparently the lump was the result of a lymph node, damaged during the latest boob job.

I didn't want to go public with the ordeal initially. I knew it was something that could help other women, urging them to get checked out, but it just didn't feel right to talk about it, especially not when poor Sarah had just revealed she was fighting so hard for her life. In fact, I didn't talk to anyone about it.

Soon Sarah became a lot less active on social media for obvious reasons and disappeared from the public eye to fight her battle privately. In the meantime statistics were brought to my attention that showed that overall the cancer rates had dropped thanks to the pandemic, but that was because people weren't getting checked out. People were dying without even being diagnosed!

That was when I went on Steph's Packed Lunch, the Channel 4 show, to tell my story.

Those statistics had scared the hell out of me. Even Sarah herself had left it too late. If I had a platform to talk about it, I should.

For anyone who watched the interview on the show, you'd think I was fine. You wouldn't even know there was a problem with me, but deep down, I was a mess. My anxiety was through the roof.

And that was just the start. I know for a fact I've not been right since.

# Health Anxiety

*****

It was two weeks before my aunt Angela died when my health anxiety really, really began to kick in. I started having these horrifically dark thoughts. I couldn't shake them. I started thinking George was going to come back, give DJ cancer and take her away from me. As a result I irrationally wouldn't let DJ leave my side. I even had her sleep in the bed with me and Ryan because I was so convinced something was going to happen to her. I'd wake in the night, panting and sweating and struggling to catch my breath after another nightmare. I was having severe panic attacks.

One night I sat bolt upright in bed with a gasp.

"What is it, Kerry?" Ryan asked, blinking in the darkness through bleary eyes.

"Someone's going to die," I said. "I can feel it. Something bad is about to happen."

He sighed. "No one's going to die. Everything will be alright."

He was trying to sound positive but I know Ryan, and I know full well he was getting freaked out by the way I was behaving. He sat me down the next morning.

"It would be good for you to speak to someone about how you're feeling," he told me gently. "Someone who could help."

With that kind encouragement, the next day I went to my doctor, who had known me for years. He told me he'd never seen me in a state like that.

"I think I'm having a nervous breakdown," I told him through tears. "Since the lump, I've not been right. I keep thinking George is going to kill DJ from beyond the grave! I have this vision of someone I love dying! I can't take it anymore!"

He listened intently but he must have thought I was mad. Well, it's not normal behaviour is it? People have been sectioned for less. Only I wasn't mad. Because two weeks later, my darling Aunty Angela died, after years of fighting her addictions.

Was that me being intuitive? Psychic? Because we later found out that she began to die a fortnight before she actually did. She had become poorly, stopped eating and was literally wasting away and no one knew. She fell and banged her head – and later checked herself out of hospital, a stupid thing for her to have done – and while all that was happening I was having these panic attacks about losing someone.

I hadn't spoken to her for a couple of years when she passed away. She had come to live with me down south when she was really struggling, back when George had been arrested for the taser possession. She was at death's door then and I helped get her sober.

But after six weeks of sobriety she went back up north and fell off the wagon. It was so frustrating for me to see, and we ended up falling out over it, which is so hypocritical of me, considering my past struggles. I know what it's like to be an addict, and I know what it's like to be the family member of an addict. And I know I handled it wrong.

Angela was more than my aunty. She was my sister. There's only ten years between us, we shared a bedroom growing up and I wanted to be her. When we were little I absolutely idolised her. She was so pretty, so fun, our Ange. She was everything.

So her death hit me terribly hard. Even now I can't talk about it. Not even to me mum. It doesn't feel real, she was so young, she still had so much to live for.

I couldn't go and see her at the Chapel of Rest. I couldn't

stand there, looking at someone so young, so special, lying there, so soon after my husband was in the exact same spot.

George and Angela, both so loved by me, both gone within 18 months of each other.

I've got such a fear of ageing and it's tied into my fear of death. I don't want to die. And with old age comes death! It's another thing that affects me when it comes to having a child with Ryan. As it stands DJ won't have had as much time with me as the others when it's my time to go, which is probably why I'm always mollycoddling her. I keep thinking I'll be dead in forty years and the kids will be without a mother. And even writing this down I'm suddenly nervous, how have I only got forty Christmases left?!

It's mad because I never used to be like this. I swear it's because of George and Angela going so suddenly. Yes I know they had issues, George with drugs, Angela with alcohol, but I never ever thought they were going to die the way they did.

With George we all used to say it was inevitable that he'd get murdered or end up back in jail, but I never truly thought he'd go so suddenly. When it actually happened – he just died. And the anger I had towards him was so intense, there was no closure. After everything he'd put us through, what was it all for? What did any of it matter? Apart from giving me DJ and inner strength I never realised I had, I wonder what on earth we went through it all for?

I feel like as a result it's messed my head up when it comes to the way I view death. It's making it hard to live in the moment. Every job opportunity I get, I'm terrified I'm going to lose it. I keep my phone on silent so I manage to avoid calls, as every call I seem to get is bad news. I'm just waiting for the other shoe to drop. I can't seem to enjoy my life to its full capacity because I'm so scared of it being taken away.

*****

It wasn't long after Angela went that Sarah Harding passed away.

I cried my eyes out when I saw the news. She was a lot of fun, a really bubbly, sweet girl who had everything to live for. We were both bridesmaids at Katie Price's wedding to Peter Andre, so in a sense we shared a little bit of celebrity history. I remember she was on amazing form that day, madly in love with Calum Best at the time and really up for a laugh. She reminded me of myself so much.

The last time I saw her was at David Gest's funeral in 2016. She wasn't in the best place if I'm honest, I think she was at a low point and a bit disillusioned with fame, even though she'd won Celebrity Big Brother just a few weeks before. It was clear the public loved her and it looks as though by all accounts she'd got herself back on track before her diagnosis. But I still feel sad that that was the last time we met up. I wish I'd been able to share a cuppa and have a chat with her before she died. I would've told her how brave she was, what an inspiration she'd been to so many women and, as a fellow girl bander, how bloody talented she was!

It wasn't to be. It's the same for David, another one gone too soon. He was my best mate for a while. We first met when I was married to Mark Croft and he just fell in love with me. I gave him my number and he would ring me at all hours. He actually stood by me when my management didn't bother, this huge, powerful figure in the music industry, once married to Liza Minnelli, who had my back no matter what.

I met so many amazing people through him.

I remember going for a meal with Smokey Robinson, would you believe.

I'll never forget the call from David.

"Honey, Smokey's in town and I've told him all about you. You two have to meet. We'll be at the Dorchester, wear something nice."

I thought it was a joke. This was too good to be true, surely? But David wasn't messing about.

"See you there?"

"I'll be there," I replied, slightly breathless, as I realised I was about to spend an evening with one of the most important, legendary singers in the history of music.

I got dolled up in my finest and arrived at the Dorchester in a taxi. Because of the way I am and how I see myself as that young girl from a council estate, I felt like a prostitute! I was convinced people were gonna ask me how much I charged, arriving at this posh hotel in my gladrags.

David came out to greet me.

"Dave, honestly, what am I doing here?" I asked.

"He's desperate to meet you darling, Smokey's heard all about you," he replied in that unmistakable slow, American drawl.

Next thing I know, the lift opened and out walked Smokey Robinson, arms outstretched, a big grin on his chops. "Kerreeeeeeeee!" he beamed as he came towards me. "I've heard so much about you!"

As you can imagine, I was barely able to speak.

He was there with his wife and daughter and we all had a

drink before dinner, the whole time I was struggling to steady my shaking hands.

David was a huge gambler and we ended up at a casino restaurant in London, somewhere near the Mayfair hotel. We were sat round this table, Smokey facing me directly, his wife next to him and David at the end. We ordered seabass for the group and, me being me, went along with it even though to be honest I didn't have a clue what it was. Anyway, I'm sitting there and David asks Smokey, "Did you go to Whitney's funeral? Did you see Diana (Ross?) Beautiful service." It was surreal being sat there listening to these legends talk about legends in such a 'normal' way.

Smokey turned to me, "David tells me you're in a band, what's it's called, Atomic something?"

"Oh no, Smokey that was ages ago, I'm not really a great singer or anything!" I spluttered. I was putting myself down thanks to an awful case of imposter syndrome. I didn't want him to think I was better than I was, even though I could still belt out a tune.

Smokey wasn't the only A-lister David tried to hook me up with. He then put me on the phone to Katherine Jackson – Michael Jackson's actual mother.

"'Ello, love" I said as breezily as I could.

Again, the response in that soft US accent. "Kerry, I've heard so much about you!"

"Oh thank you!" I replied, not having a clue what else I could possibly say to that. I don't think either of us had much more to say after that, in fact. It was a truly bizarre, short, but incredible interaction. Coincidentally I would end up having meals with the remaining members of the Jackson Five when they'd come to the UK thanks to David. My George and Tito in particular got on like a house on fire.

David was so much fun. We once went to Memphis for ten days, on his dollar. He wanted to film us doing a scripted comedy pilot with a few artists such as Peabo Bryson and Candi Staton, another icon who famously sang Young Hearts Run Free.

One day I was shopping in Macy's with Candy having a right old giggle. Then before I knew it, we're sitting in a Chrysler on our way to a gospel church. Candy wanted me to witness an authentic gospel experience, and I was thrilled to go along.

As promised, it was incredible to be there, but when she got me up at the altar to help her sing You Got The Love – oh my God, I've never known anything like it. It was unbelievable. And it was all filmed! Nothing ever came of it, I don't think it ever saw the light of day but I do have a DVD copy somewhere. I just can't bring myself to watch it. Seeing David on the screen, it makes me too sad. I hate the fact he's not here any more. The banter we used to have – he had such a naughty sense of humour. I used to tease him by asking him if Liza had given him crabs and he'd be crying with laughter. He really thought I was dead funny and he was so proud of me, he'd take me everywhere and introduce me to anyone and everyone.

It was through David that I met Dennis Graham, probably better known as Drake's dad. Yep, *that* Drake. He's another great guy and we once spent an evening doing karaoke together. We belted out a mean version of Sittin' on the Dock of the Bay. Even now, we're in touch. He messaged me on Instagram recently and we had a good laugh remembering David.

It's definitely true that I'm always looking for father figures, or I certainly was growing up. But David wasn't like that. Instead he was a fun older brother. He was like Peter Pan. He was such a handful, a real cheeky guy who got away with murder, but he was such good fun!

When it came to father figures, famously my most high profile one was Max Clifford. And of course he fell from grace in spectacular fashion. After being found guilty of numerous sex offences against young girls, he died in prison in 2017, at the age of 74.

I was told he'd died just minutes before I was due to go on stage at panto and I was gutted. It was such a conflicting feeling, because I will always, one hundred percent, believe and support his victims – for what he did to those poor girls he deserved every minute of that jail time.

But he was also always kind to me. I never, ever saw that side of him and so for me to sit here and tell my truth, I have to be honest. I could only ever judge him on the way he was with me, and he cared for me and loved me like a daughter. I named my son after him, for God's sake.

Since his death I've been offered huge sums of money to spill the beans on my own experiences with him. People assume I must have been groomed, or accosted or made to do things against my will.

But that was never the case. I'm not for a second defending what he did to those poor girls but he was never ever once inappropriate with me. And when it was revealed in a TV documentary just how depraved he was, I sobbed like a baby. I was gutted. I imagine it's like the horror of finding out your father's a paedophile. You're disgusted and saddened, but he's still your father.

Well, Max was like that to me.

I met him via Brian McFadden. Westlife had him on a retainer for £30k a month, but he took on my PR for free. Yes, if I landed a gig or some work he'd take his 20 per cent, but he never charged me for looking after me.

When Brian cheated on me I was so sure Max would stay on his side. Instead he called me up and said, "I think it's disgusting what he's done to you Kerry. I'll look after you." And he did. He dumped Brian and remained loyal to me. He even gave me away at my second wedding, despite warning me, rightly, that I probably shouldn't go through with it.

We had the sort of relationship where I could tell him to eff-off – I once remember Coleen Nolan stood there, her mouth completely agape after listening to me tell him where to go.

"Who the hell speaks to Max Clifford like that?!" she said, unable to hide her admiration.

My fond memories of who he was with me will never change. He would wine and dine me and take me out with celebrities. I had great experiences because of Max.

Clearly he was a bastard and when you watch the documentary you can hear his voice on tapes, talking to and about the young girls he was grooming. There's no question he was a narcissist and what he did there was evil.

But I can't suddenly change my feelings because of something he did that was completely separate from me. He treated me like his daughter. I can only ever tell my truth and my truth is that I'd get a hug from Max Clifford and feel completely safe. I know now that wasn't everyone's experience. I understand these poor, poor women who suffered at his hands had every right to tell their truth and that truth is just as valid as mine.

It always crossed my mind whether or not I should write to

him in prison. I didn't in the end, and that was probably for the best. I'm not even sure what I'd have said. I wouldn't have offered support for what he did, but knowing he saved my bacon on so many occasions, I almost wanted to know he was ok.

I did want to go to the funeral, but my management discouraged me from going, which I understand.

I think the bottom line is, I struggle to link what he did to those girls with what he did for me. He was instrumental in my fame. To this day, I still don't know why he singled me out to look after. Maybe after I won the jungle and me and Brian went through such a public divorce, he saw pound signs. Maybe I was always his cash cow? Or maybe he genuinely cared about me. Whatever it was he was never, ever inappropriate to me, and that's *my* truth.

And I can't change what Clifford did to those girls. I just hope they find peace, especially now he's gone.

# 15

# Daddy Issues

My kids are my entire world. I'd do anything for them. But one thing does frustrate me when it comes to my children, and that's this narrative that I in some way 'co-parent' Molly and Lilly with Brain McFadden.

Let me get something clear – I'm on fine terms with Brian these days but there's certainly no 'co' in our parenting! I've done all the hard work myself.

I know for Molly and Lilly it's a different story, though. I know for a fact they wish they were closer to their dad, but at this stage in their lives I'm not sure it's going to happen. Especially as Brian now has a baby daughter, Ruby, with his partner Danielle Parkinson, who I should point out is one of the loveliest women in the world. I genuinely have a girl crush on her. Say what you will about Brian, he's got good taste in baby mamas.

Seeing their dad's closeness to his new family unit is something that must be tough for Molly and Lilly. They're not jealous of Ruby, in fact they completely adore her, but it must be hard for them to see Brian be so doting over his youngest daughter. It's hard for me to see it. It breaks my heart in fact. I suppose I didn't realise quite how difficult it must have been for them – but it's something I can't resolve. All I can do is be there for my girls, the effort has to come from Brian's side.

Truthfully I would love nothing more than for me, Brian, Lilly and Molly to go for a meal together. For the girls to see their parents in the same room as each other, acting like grown-ups. We've never actually been in the same room since the kids were little and even now they get freaked out at the thought of us even being married in the first place!

I really feel there's room for improvement when it comes to all of our relationships.

Danielle has been incredible in that respect, as she seems to have made Brian more approachable. I think she's far too good for him and I hope he knows how lucky he is! But she has changed him.

If it wasn't for Danielle, me and Brian wouldn't have the tiny, tiny morsel of relationship we do have. For instance, I'm comfortable now messaging him to ask what sort of guitar is best to buy for Molly, seeing as he knows more about that kind of thing than I do.

I'm not sure we'd have been able to have that exchange before Danielle came on the scene. She seems to know how to get through to him when it comes to me and my girls. She's so relaxed about our family dynamics, and that seems to rub off on Brian.

Although not always, clearly.

I remember when she was born I bought Ruby a Moschino baby tracksuit and I got Brian and Danielle some Jo Malone candles and sprays. But yet he didn't even get Lilly a card for her 19th birthday the same year. No present, nothing. Which I'm not surprised at, but it does sting a bit, knowing that would hurt Lilly.

And on her 18th Brian promised he'd buy her a car but he never did. He gave her some cash instead.

The kids always come to me when they need something, I have to tell them to ask their dad too on occasion but the truth is, they're more comfortable asking me. It's always me sorting stuff out, when a lot of the time it should be him or at the very least a joint decision between the pair of us.

✳✳✳✳✳

Don't get me wrong, me and Brian are fine, but I do get upset when he upsets my girls, unintentionally or not. When they come to me complaining, which they rarely do (because they know I'll kick off) – that's when I get frustrated. It hurts me to see my babies hurt. I know how it feels, not having a dad and I hate the fact they have one, but he's not as invested as he perhaps could be.

Brian lived out in Australia for a large portion of their childhood, and it was never enough to just be in the background, sending the odd text. The bottom line is, I did the parents evenings, I did the sports days. Brian never ever went to any of those events.

So it says a lot then, that out of the three of my baby daddies, Brian's the best! (Mind you, one of them's dead, so he's not got a lot of competition!)

But I can't have resentment towards him. I just can't. I've been there, done that and I know for a fact it ends up eating you alive. Just being the bigger person is sometimes enough. I want Brian to be happy. Obviously I want him to trip down the stairs now and again too, but on the whole I really wish everyone well and that we could all get on. I want everyone living their best lives.

People sometimes ask if I'm jealous that Brian moved on, somehow forgetting we haven't been together for decades. I have no love towards Brian but equally there's no animosity either.

What I'm left with is this enormous frustration for my girls. When I see the hurt in my babies' eyes, that's when I get angry. Brian doesn't always understand that. He doesn't get it.

He's their biological dad, but he hasn't played that all-important father figure role in their lives growing up. Not in the way that George had and Ryan does now. And I'll never take that away from George. For all his faults, he was more of a dad to those girls than Brian ever was. And I'm not having a go at Brian, he'd be the first one to put his hands up and admit he wasn't around nearly as much as he should have been when they were growing up.

I'm almost certain it's an age thing with Brian. He's a different man now he's a lot older and maybe that's why he seems so much more devoted to Ruby than he ever was to our kids. You have to remember we were babies ourselves when we had Molly and Lilly – but that never diminished my love for my first-borns, so I'd hope he would be the same.

I've been there for those girls in the good times and the bad times, and yes, I'll admit, some of those bad times are down to me. But I've always been there, no matter what.

When it comes to Danielle, Molly and Lilly (and Ryan and the rest of the kids) absolutely adore her. She was different from the start. She was much more keen to be involved with the girls than any of Brian's other exes, and I was happy to have her be part of our strange, blended family set-up.

The first time we met was when Brian brought her to my panto and we got together backstage. I was dressed as the witch (in character, of course!) He took a picture of the pair of us and posted it with the caption, 'When the love of your life meets your evil ex-wife.'

It was all quite tongue-in-cheek and I played along and it felt like a breakthrough. The press loved it of course. And it goes to show just how easy going Danielle is.

But before I'd even met her the girls acknowledged that she'd changed their dad. She made him more responsive to them, somehow. She used to be a teacher, so I think she knows how to talk to kids, she gets them, and she's proven to be an amazing stepmum-to-be to my girls.

I hope as everyone continues to get older, Ruby included, that Molly and Lilly are able to be close to that side of the family. They will always have me, no matter what, but I'd love for them to have a stronger bond with their father.

And hopefully in time, they will.

# 16

# A Stranger Calls

And speaking of fathers… It was late October in 2021 when I got the shock of my life. It's not every day your dead husband's biological dad reaches out to make contact with you and at a point where I finally felt settled, it came as a huge surprise.

It was a chilly day. I remember being wrapped up in my jumper, cup of tea in hand suffering from the after effects of a nasty tummy bug, when I sat down to go through my message requests on social media. It's something I do most days. You know how it is, a company might be offering me a freebie and I wouldn't wanna miss it! Then, I spotted something that caught my eye.

A short, succinct request, accompanied by a picture that looked strangely familiar. Hauntingly so. I hovered over the message, able to see the contents but not opening it fully so that the sender – who, for the purposes of keeping his identity secret I'll call Marvin – couldn't see I'd read it.

'Hi Kerry. I apologise for contacting you this way. You don't know me but allow me to introduce myself. My name *is Marvin, I'm the natural father of your ex, George. I just found out my son has passed away. And I understand that you had a daughter together. Therefore, on compassionate grounds, would you consider my requests to get to know my granddaughter. Best wishes.'*

I froze. My stomach churned and I thought for a second I was going to throw up. I peered at the picture on the message a little longer. It was the spitting image of George. I might as well have been contacted by his ghost via DM.

Now this was too much to take in. This was so messed up. I ran to the toilet, clutching my stomach and must have sat there in my bathroom for what felt like hours. I just wept, the photo of Marvin now etched in my mind, the likeness uncanny.

"I can't keep crying over you George," I sobbed to the invisible spirit of my dead husband. "What am I supposed to do with this message? How can you still be haunting me like this?!"

It was so heavy on me. And coincidentally I'd just filmed a TV show called Fame in the Family. It's a programme in which you find out where you came from. During filming I was given a picture of my biological granddad, which as you can imagine was a huge deal for me, as someone who never knew a large chunk of her family.

So now, for Marvin to get in touch so soon after I discovered my biological granddad…it's almost like things were happening for a reason. Otherwise it was all too coincidental, surely? Mind you, even thinking that way didn't make it easier to digest.

A couple of days went by but the message was weighing so heavily on me. Eventually, after stewing on it for what felt like an eternity, I sent one back.

'Just seeing your face is like George coming back,' I wrote.

'But this is a lot!!!! How do I know you are who you say you are?' Marvin responded almost immediately.

'Thanks for your reply. Please don't be distressed or worried, I won't cause any anxiety for you and your daughter, myself or any of our close relatives,' he wrote.

He went on to explain more. George wasn't adopted until he was two. By all accounts Marvin, who is Nigerian, fought to no avail to keep his baby boy.

The message continued (with names changed) – 'I was married to Maureen in 1978 and we had three children. Lisa, George and David. David died as a baby. We all lived in Liverpool, we have family who can confirm my identity and I am prepared to show you my passports and documents to prove who I am. Please rest assured you are dealing with George's real dad. May the peace of the Lord be with us all. Thank you for your time and may God bless you and your family.'

It was a thoughtful, thorough message from a God-fearing, church-going African man who's rich in his culture.

I replied equally as quickly.

'I'm sure you understand, this is a lot to take in. You look so alike,' I said. 'I'm so sorry you've only just found out about his passing. Please forgive me, I'm finding this rather difficult.'

It turns out Marvin had only found out about George's death via Google. As soon as he saw the news report, he knew it was his son. He had to sit his family down and explain that he had a dead son and a little granddaughter they never knew about.

It's mad to think that after the extensive tabloid interest in mine and George's relationship, Marvin had never seen him before. He wasn't aware at all. He has no interest in celebrity news.

He responded, still via direct message.

'I know it's difficult for you. I have four other children, and they were angry with me when I told them. My youngest daughter wants to reach out to you. Believe me, my heart is aching and I'm in tears as I'm writing this to you.'

Well, as you can imagine, I was sobbing as I read it too.

Marvin continued, writing, 'I have three sons who look just like George. This life can be so cruel, no father should know of the death of any of his children. I'm a laid back sort of man, I wasn't going to write to you, but since my other daughter pushed me to write, shall we talk? I think it may help. I'm really sorry it's come to this, but you'll soon realise all of us are affected by the loss of George.'

This was tricky. I wasn't ready to have a face to face conversation with him. It was too sudden – after all this time, after all my progress, I felt like I was back in a room with my George. It was like he had a hold on me all over again, and that's no slight on Marvin. It's just the way I felt.

I took to my keyboard and began to tentatively type out a response, desperate not to offend but conscious I had to look after myself too.

'I really don't want to insult, but I'm extremely cautious when it comes to people I don't know, especially when it comes to my baby girl,' I wrote back.

'This is all so very overwhelming. You must understand the questions going around in my head over the fact you never made any contact with George when he was alive. I need time to sit on this, please. I do hope you understand.'

I left it at that. I couldn't say any more. I certainly couldn't commit to meeting him at this stage.

As expected, Marvin sent a message back straight away.

'I really do understand. I did try and find George. I'll leave you alone now so you can take this all in, but please do all you can to help stop a very bad situation getting hopeless. If you don't mind I'll contact you again in a week's time, but please feel free to contact me at any time. Stay blessed.'

I replied, 'You have so many answers for DJ that I can't give her. Reading your message and seeing your picture this morning is heartbreaking. Just wishing George himself was here to read this. It's been so tough. I'll say goodnight for now.'

*****

So there it was. The doors of communication had been opened to a man I never, ever thought I'd hear from or get to know. But he was DJ's grandfather and that would never change. I waited until the next morning before reaching out again. Somehow, after a night's rest I felt stronger, more together. It was always the way.

I began typing and breezily tried to restart the conversation with Marvin by asking where he was based.

He replied, 'I know it must be difficult for you, it's been difficult for me to get my head around what happened to my fine son.'

And there's me thinking, 'He doesn't know the half of it'.

'I should have been there for him,' Marvin continued. 'Blood runs deep. I'm now living in Buckinghamshire, though strangely in the past few weeks I've been thinking of moving back to Liverpool. I'm willing to travel up north if you want to meet to make it easier.'

# A Stranger Calls

For some reason the idea of coming face to face with George's father, in the flesh, panicked me.

'Let's start with Facetime,' I replied, cautiously. 'Just me and you first.'

He agreed. We sent a few more messages back and forth, I watched them spring to the screen through tears, the whole experience was so incredibly overwhelming, but at the back of my mind I kept thinking about DJ. About how much it would mean to her, as a mixed race child, to have that link back to her father's heritage. To know that side of her family now her own daddy wasn't there to provide her with the answers I just knew she'd need growing up.

I didn't tell a soul what had happened. In hindsight perhaps I should have spoken about it, but instead I shouldered the burden of this bizarre situation all by myself for at least a week.

I didn't know how to deal with it. There were so many factors to figure out. This was my estranged, dead husband's biological dad, how messed up is that?! I had to get my head straight before I sat down and told Ryan.

He told me I had to do the right thing and tell DJ. As always, my amazing Ryan was absolutely right. With his encouragement I took the next step, and, just a few days after that first message from Marvin, we Facetimed.

I was so unbelievably nervous, but, oh my, the shock I had when he appeared on the screen! It was George. The image. I couldn't speak – it was like the ghost of my dead husband was right there in the flesh, looking at me, talking to me.

What's more, Marvin was the image of DJ. And that also took me by surprise.

He's a jolly man, he spoke in a broken English accent, he told me about George's mum, Maureen.

He had met her when he was just 19 and moved in with her and her dad when he came to settle in England.

Now obviously I never met Maureen, she's dead now, but George would tell me stories about her, how she had mental health issues and drug problems.

But by all accounts, Marvin stuck by her and together they had three babies, including George. Now, this is the reason I knew I was talking to George's biological dad. George was born with six fingers on each hand, and Marvin knew that. In fact he told me that was one of the reasons why Maureen, suffering from poor mental health at the time, went to give him up for adoption. She was convinced he was a monster.

Now, this part of George's story I never knew. I knew he was adopted and I knew that his dad tried to fight for him, but I didn't know it was Maureen, in her vulnerable state, who had made that final decision based on George's *fingers*.

Their little boy was adopted when it became clear that Marvin couldn't afford to keep fighting for George. Financially he just couldn't do it anymore.

We spoke for an hour and a half and he was a lovely, lovely person. Very religious, very family orientated.

The day before I next went to call him, I sat DJ down first, in the knowledge I might put her on the line with him, depending on how it went.

"Did you know your daddy was adopted?" I asked her.

She looked at me with those gorgeous wide eyes. "No?"

I grabbed a piece of paper. "You know how Mummy was in a foster home growing up?"

"Yes…"

I began to scribble out a basic family tree.

"So this is your daddy's mummy and daddy, right? This mummy and daddy couldn't look after your daddy, so this mummy and daddy took him on and loved him instead!"

I carried on, to the point where I felt she understood and then I told her daddy's daddy – her biological granddad – had got in touch and would love to talk to her.

Remember she was seven years old, and this was a lot for her to take in, but as always, my little girl was strong.

"I'd like to see a picture please, Mummy."

So I showed her the profile picture from his messages. And her face lit up. I cry even now thinking about it. She wasn't upset, she wasn't scared, she was… happy. It was like she just knew instinctively who this man was.

"He looks like me!" she shrieked with delight. "And like Daddy!"

So you'd definitely like to meet him?"

"Oh yes please Mummy."

I put her on the video call at the end of a good hour and a half conversation I'd had with Marvin. DJ was shy at first, polite but a little bit nervous, but before long she was chatting away and you should've seen the tears rolling down his face as they talked.

There was something magical, if a little odd about the whole situation. Just a few days ago I didn't even know this man existed, and yet here he is, bonding with my daughter, his grandchild, over Facetime. It was a bizarre experience, but one which was obviously making DJ happy.

I suppose this was as good as the situation could possibly be at this point and I felt relieved in my decision to let her speak with him.

The next day we'd come home from a day out and DJ asked, "Mummy, can I call my granddad up and tell him about what happened today?"

I shouldn't have been surprised really. He'd made such an impression on her.

"It's a bit late today sweetheart, maybe tomorrow?"

In the meantime I had sent lots of pictures of DJ and George to Marvin, videos of them dancing together, playing, smiling. Just looking through the footage caused my stomach to knot and the tears to fall. George could be such a wonderful dad. He had so, so many faults and a real bad side, but when he was good….he was brilliant. And to see those pictures and videos and know DJ won't experience that again, it broke my heart.

But at the same time it was cathartic. It was like Marvin's reappearance, which just days ago had been the source of such terrible anxiety and fright, was now something positive. A light for my daughter and a link back to the dad she'll never grow up with.

One thing I was struggling with at this time was the fact that Max and Heidi both called George dad, too. No matter what we went through with him, they looked at him like a father figure, considering by now theirs was totally out of the picture.

It led to some tricky conversations. "Why can't we see George's dad? Isn't he our granddad too?" Max asked, when I told them about DJ's video call.

Clearly there were a lot of feelings for them all to deal with. And I was trying to navigate it so as not to mess with their little heads any more than I had to.

# A Stranger Calls

It's such a hard thing to do – would Marvin really care about two kids not related to him? I decided for the moment to keep it to just him and DJ. The next day I organised another call.

The three of us chatted for a bit, with DJ being her shy self, looking to me for answers when Marvin would ask her questions.

So I made my excuses, got up and pretended to do some cleaning. I left the room, obviously keeping my eyes and ears on her but out of her eyeshot, and watched as my little girl just lit up. Without me there she found her voice, and suddenly there was no shutting her up! She was so chatty!

Weirdly, I noticed she was a lot clingier to me and Ryan after she met her granddad. And I think it was her way of reassuring us. She's obviously completely elated that this man is in her life, but she wants us to know we haven't been forgotten as a result. It's enough to make your heart burst, really.

"I'm so happy about my granddad," she proudly announced to me shortly after.

It turns out Marvin is from a tribe in Nigeria that are featured in the Natural History Museum, which he wants to show DJ. Having six fingers on each hand is something genetic that stems from the tribe, so again that's something that DJ inherited from that side.

My baby girl is a descendant of a Nigerian tribe – it's incredible really. And I know it's something she'll want to know more about as she gets older.

For me the most rewarding part of this curveball into my life is the fact that DJ is so bloody thrilled by the developments. What's been a lot more difficult is filling Marvin in on George's death, and his life in the spotlight.

I knew I had to tell him about the fact George was famous through being with me. I also had to fill him in on the drugs, the mental health issues, the violence. But I knew I had to protect Marvin too. This lovely, polite older man.

"Your son was great, but he had a lot of demons," I tried to broach the subject gently.

Marvin told me that he got that from Maureen, his mother. He seemed to immediately understand. There was no judgement, no shock, really. It was like he just knew.

My George was a really tortured soul and I believe a lot of it came from the fact he didn't know his biological family. I know that because I felt the same way growing up. Even now I know I'm messed up because of it. George died before he ever got to meet his father, and yet here I was meeting him instead. It was so upsetting and confusing and the guilt I felt! Why was I being given an opportunity to have an audience with the man my George would've done anything to meet?

I found the whole experience so overwhelming but I knew it was best for DJ. It's a lot to deal with but there's a blessing in the fact we were getting to know him. DJ's entitled to know her culture and her history, and here's a genuine link to that for her.

I was seven when I got told the man who I thought was my dad wasn't my real dad. Seven years old. And I remember how that affected me. Could you imagine what it was like for DJ to lose her daddy when she was even younger than that?

George's death left me dealing with not just my own grief but the grief of my children too, especially DJ's. So it was an incredibly overwhelming thing to cope with, seeing her welcome Marvin into her life. I know it's a good thing – a great thing! But I'm cautious.

# A Stranger Calls

And it later turned out, maybe I had reason to be.

Not long after I connected with Marvin, I received an email from a woman claiming to be George's sister. I'm sure you can imagine how stressful it can be when all sorts of strangers start coming out of the woodwork in relation to your dead husband.

She wrote, 'I received some news tonight that I didn't expect to receive. As far as I know your husband George was my little brother George. And he's passed. I found out this news tonight, and to be honest I am very shocked. I don't know if it's appropriate to contact you, but felt it was something I needed to do.'

Oh God, here we go.

His sister seemed to have a different version of the family tree to her step dad, Marvin, even when taking the late son David out of the equation. Tellingly, she clearly wasn't a fan of Marvin's. I've changed the names in her email.

'To surprise you even more. There is four of us, not two of them,' she wrote. 'My mother (who passed away around 98/99) had four children. Kath is the eldest, Me, Lisa, then George. To think George thought he only had one sister is difficult for me to process. As I am older I remember being told George was adopted and I wouldn't be able to see him anymore. There are a couple of fathers but all the same mother.'

She went on to tell me that Marvin had no qualms about putting all the blame on Maureen for losing the children, it seems they all went into care, but in Maureen's defence, she didn't have these children alone.

'Marvin had no problem confirming my mother and her sister were prostitutes,' George's sister continued. 'He told me quite coldly that I was put into care and nobody would speak of me, that I was like some dirty shameful secret. He said he was only a student and wanted to settle down with Maureen but she was crazy. That her family was crazy and then he brought up some story about how badly he was treated by her brother or something.'

It suddenly felt like I was in the middle of some surreal soap opera, caught in a warring family who I had no idea existed a few days prior. This was all getting a bit overwhelming.

'He's painted himself as her saviour,' she continued. 'That she was mad, her family are all liars, prostitutes and thieves. That I should stay away from them. How he went looking all over Liverpool for George and Lisa and couldn't find them.'

Apparently Maureen had been in the papers for committing bigamy, but George's sister never stopped sticking up for her mum.

'When all this was going on what kind of life did my mother have?' she asked. 'Whilst in all this mess of prostitutes, liars, thieves and lost children how can Marvin be the only good person in this whole story?'

Yikes. It's clear there's a feuding family here that I suddenly wasn't sure I wanted to get involved with. Was Marvin not the kind gentleman he appeared to be? Did George's sister have an agenda of her own that I needed to stay well away from?

I suppose realistically I need to take things at face value. All I know is Marvin's tried to make an effort to be in touch with DJ and he's an essential link to her past heritage. I guess I need to go forward with a bit of caution and I won't discount the email from his step daughter completely.

I remember the amount of people who would dismiss me based on press reports and public opinion and it wouldn't be fair on me to do the same to Marvin. I'm going to keep keeping myself to myself and if DJ wants to see him, I'll keep an open mind.

As I write this, Marvin has gone quiet again, I've not heard from him in a while and I'm not going to chase. Perhaps the step daughter got to him? Maybe he wasn't being entirely truthful about his background and now he's backtracking?

Who knows, but I'm going to wait and see how it pans out. I so want DJ to have all the answers he could provide her, but I won't get her hopes up in case he's gone for good too, just like her Daddy.

I don't want her to deal with another man disappearing forever.

# 17

## Cat Fight

When I was a little girl, stuck between council houses and foster homes, I dreamed of becoming famous. But more specifically, a pop star. When you're a teen and the likes of Eternal and The Spice Girls are on every radio station and magazine cover going, it's hard not to get sucked into the marketing of it all – I loved it. And what's more I had charisma, I was stripping a bit so I knew I could dance, and, believe it or not, I could hold a tune! I also had the looks. The blonde hair, the big boobs, the small waist. I always knew I could be just like Posh, Baby, Ginger, Sporty and Scary, staring out from the cover of Smash Hits.

And, just like that, one day it happened for me. Atomic Kitten were discovered by Andy McCluskey, who was the lead singer of Orchestral Manoeuvres in the Dark, or OMD as they're more widely known. You'll know their big hit, Enola Gay, which soundtracks just about every advert and TV drama set in the 80s going.

I was in the original line-up, alongside Liz McClarnon and Heidi Range, who was later replaced with Natasha Hamilton after Heidi and Liz had a bust-up (Heidi went on to be in the Sugababes), and for a significant period of time we were happy. We toured the world! We wined and dined with megastars, we dated (and in my case married) boybanders, we had number one singles and I loved every single minute of it.

That is, until I fell pregnant with our Molly in 2001, just three years after the Kittens were formed.

All I ever wanted was to have a baby and a family and it was a no brainer for me to stop work when it happened. I had made my own money through the band, and I was already looking forward to a life of domesticity in my big mansion with my prince and our daughter.

Of course we all know it didn't quite work out that way, and sadly when things went wrong between me and Brian, I couldn't just change my mind, flip a switch and go back to the Kittens.

I was replaced by Jenny Frost and she and the girls continued on and had relative success.

Meanwhile, I was away for the next decade, winning I'm A Celebrity, getting cheated on, meeting and marrying Mark Croft – and we all know how that ended up – but I was always itching to get back on stage.

So when the opportunity came up to rejoin the band in 2012, to appear in the Big Reunion with the original line up, I jumped at it.

I was told by Tash that Jenny was somehow embarrassed and didn't want anything to do with the show, so luckily for me, I got the call! And boy am I eternally grateful it panned out that way.

*****

Ever since I rejoined the Kittens I felt like I had imposter syndrome. It wasn't just that I'd been out of the game so long, it was a matter of my own confidence in my talent. I always felt I wasn't as good as the other two.

Tash in particular has a phenomenal voice and I know my vocals are weak in comparison. I'm not too proud to say I know I was picked for the band because of my personality and tits!

It didn't help that the girls would make jokes about turning off my mic when we'd sing. Things like that do stay with you, and it used to knock my confidence a lot. That said, I was always at my most comfortable on stage, and, over the next few years we would gig and do one off festivals and I used to love every second of it.

It was February 2017 and we were on a big tour over in Australia, the first we'd done in a long while. Liz, who was terrified of flying, wouldn't get on a plane, so the Liberty X singer Michelle Heaton took her place, as she often did if we needed to do a long haul journey.

Part of the tour took us to New Zealand, which is where things started to go wrong.

Michelle has since been very open about her fight against alcoholism, but at the time we didn't realise she had problems, we just knew she liked a tipple, and she and Tash would often be out on the lash while we were on the road. I can't handle my ale so I don't drink very often. In fact during that whole Australian tour I never really went out on the piss. I went out alone mostly. I'd go and climb the Sydney Harbour Bridge on my own while the girls would be off at boozy yacht parties getting wasted. I didn't do any of that, because it had been so long since I'd been away with a band, I wanted to soak it all in.

# Cat Fight

Anyway, we're in New Zealand and we'd been on this ferry to take us to Waiheke Island. Drinks had been flowing throughout the day and Michelle had managed to get absolutely shit-faced. It turned into a right palaver.

Upon returning to dry land, Tash and I had to help Michelle out of the car to get her to her hotel room. Michelle was being sick everywhere, she was upset, crying and we ended up having to call an ambulance. It was a lot, but as always, we dealt with it and hoped the next morning would be a bit more drama-free, if not hangover-free.

But that wasn't quite the case.

The next day we're in a pub, when our tour manager took us aside.

"Girls, there's been some bad news. There's pap pictures of Michelle being sick – they're all over the press at home."

I was gobsmacked. "We're in the middle of New Zealand – how the bloody hell would a pap know where we are?"

Now I've been very open about the fact I set up my own paparazzi pictures, I use an agency I trust and whatever we sell to the papers, we then split the money. To me it's a savvy business move – why should someone else take photos of me, use my image and I not benefit from it?

The point being, I would be completely honest and open if I'd have had anything to do with the pap getting those unflattering shots of Michelle. But I didn't. I would never, ever have a pap take pics of me with another celeb without that person's knowledge. Ever.

So there we were in this pub. And everyone was horrified by the release of these pictures. It's not the best look for Michelle, or any of us in fact. We're in our late thirties at this point, and it makes us all look like we're out of control. As someone in the band, especially someone who'd been playing it safe all tour, I was pretty angry about how it could reflect on me personally.

"How the hell did that pap know where we were?" I asked the girls. "I don't even bloody well know where we are!"

Incidentally when I clocked the shots, I realised there's one picture where Tash is looking directly at the camera. What was that about?

Tash turned around to me and said in that heavy Liverpool accent of hers, "Are you sure you've not tipped them off Kerry? Coz you had your pap at the airport…"

I was fuming.

"What do you mean 'am I sure?!' I think I'd remember if I'd told a pap where we were!" I spat back.

She kept looking at me. "Are you sure?"

"What are you insinuating, Tash? The amount of times I've been set up by mates when it comes to dodgy papped shots of me, you'd think I'd set up my own band members? Are YOU sure, Tash?!"

She rolled her eyes and I saw red. We got into a huge fight. I'm not proud of the fact it turned physical but I was absolutely fuming that she was accusing me of doing something I absolutely didn't do.

Honestly, I was going mental. I kicked off in front of everyone. They ended up locking me out of the pub, so I tried to break the door down to get back in. I was absolutely furious.

I could hear Tash crying and screaming all sorts back at me, but I was so angry I could barely see straight. I wonder to this day if it was actually her.

But here's the thing, like it always is with sisters, it was soon forgotten. And the next day, after we'd slept on it, Tash and I made up. It was like it had never happened.

After all, it wasn't the first time we'd fought. As a group we were always getting into scraps and screaming matches behind the scenes. It's hard not to when you spend that amount of time with people in such an intense environment, like a tour.

I remember once having a huge blow out with Liz McClarnon, when she punched me in the back of the head after a row. I got my own back by stamping on her feet while we performed Whole Again live on SM:TV. It's little things like that, really.

To be honest I didn't think much more of the New Zealand spat and when we got back to England I'd basically forgotten about it. We cracked on with gigging and doing what we do.

But looking back, I'm starting to think Tash didn't forget quite as easily.

A few months passed and life was going on. I was away from George for good and feeling stronger than ever and enjoying some of the perks of celebrity life, including a comedy gig I did as part of a drag queen contest in Manchester that October.

It was a bit of stand-up for me, and I was in my element. When I'm on stage I'm dead funny – well I think I am – you see, that's one thing I do pride myself on. I use quick witted put downs as humour.

Up on stage the Queens referred to Atomic Kitten as 'Explosive Pussy.' It was all a bit vulgar and in bad taste – but hilarious. I was then asked what Tash was really like, and, to take the piss and get my own joke in there I replied, "Oh she's a toxic c**t".

Let me explain how I got there – Kitten…pussy….c**t. In NO WAY was I actually calling Tash a c**t.

Of course it was all meant in good humour and if you'd been in the audience you would've known that straight away from my delivery.

But when it's written down in a headline the next day all over the papers and taken completely out of context, it doesn't look quite as funny.

Instead the old press tropes came out. 'Kerry has foul-mouthed meltdown on stage!!' screamed the tabloid websites.

I've always used my humour as a defence mechanism and I love being savage. Why can someone like Joan Rivers be considered hilarious when that's her form of comedy, but when it's mine, I'm attacked for it?

Anyway, I can stand here now and I say I would never, ever have meant it seriously. I loved Tash more than anything, I've been through things with that girl that I've never been through with anyone else and I genuinely looked at her like my sister. Of course I don't actually think she's a toxic c**t.

She never said anything about it. So part of me thought it was all ok, she knew my humour and if I'm honest I didn't give it much more thought.

It was a couple of weeks later and we were doing a performance at Butlin's. But I just knew from the moment we saw Tash that day that the atmosphere had changed. She was being off with me and Michelle (who had stepped in for Liz again), and she just came out with it.

"I need a break from this," she said. "I don't wanna do this anymore."

I was shocked but at the same time I wasn't exactly heartbroken. I knew it wasn't the end of the band or a long term thing, at that point I figured Tash just needed a bit of time out, which I totally respected. She had four kids, she was probably done with being away from home on the road. I respected her decision and told her gently, "We're not going anywhere, take all the time you need."

The next thing I know, I see a headline saying that Atomic Kitten had split up. Well, this was news to me. As far as I was concerned this was a break, nothing more.

I attempted to clarify things on social media. 'We're just doing separate things for a while,' I wrote.

I was unsettled by it, but I put it all down to a mistake and tried not to think about it any more, until a couple of weeks later I saw that Tash and Liz were still gigging. Just without me.

What the hell?! Apparently they *did* want to continue! Only not with me!

A fan sent me a DM saying they couldn't wait to see me performing with the girls at an upcoming gig. They'd attached a picture of the promo poster which featured all three of us on it. They were still using my image on the posters to sell tickets – but hadn't invited me to the bloody gig!

I was shocked but I couldn't get hold of anyone to find out what exactly was going on. No one would return my texts. I had no idea what was happening or where I stood. I was so, so upset and even to this day I still don't know what happened there.

It breaks my heart because I'm so super proud of the band.

But I know they never want me to be on stage with them again. Ever.

*****

We never spoke in person again. The only time there was even a tiny bit of communication was when I got a voice message from Tash after George died. I replied immediately but didn't hear back, and now she's blocked me on Instagram.

I've sent Liz a message telling her how much I loved her and how there's no hard feelings and that I wish them all the best, but that was completely ignored as well.

Still, to this day, I don't know what I did wrong. If Tash was genuinely offended by my 'toxic c\*\*t' joke, she could've called, I would've straightened it out immediately.

Atomic Kitten will always have a special place in my heart, and I will be forever proud of us. I find it really sad that I don't have the girls to walk down memory lane with now. We experienced so much together. We were unknown, we grafted together, we did the nightclubs, we travelled the world. My DJ will never get to see me perform on stage with the girls and that makes me so terribly sad.

I watched the Whole Again resurgence during the Euros, when the song became a bit of an unofficial anthem for the England football team, with such sadness. I'd have loved to be a part of that, but of course I wasn't invited to be.

Sometimes I look back at poor Sarah Harding and I wonder to myself, if I were to die, would Liz and Tash start crying and want to come to my funeral? Would they start gushing about what a wonderful friend I'd been and how much they're going to miss me?

I'm a grown woman, I'm a mother of five, and this playground squabbling is bullshit. I can't live with hate. I have to forgive and let things go, or it'll eat me up.

Don't get me wrong, I'll speak my truth and I will do so unapologetically, but I don't wish the girls anything but love.

# Cat Fight

I'm sad and envious. What I wouldn't give to be back on stage with them. There's no better feeling than being in front of an audience with your mates singing songs and doing dance routines. I'd be there in a heartbeat if they wanted me back.

I still speak to Michelle now and then but she doesn't really give me any indication as to what happened. I don't know if it was the New Zealand bust up or the 'c**t' comment that sent Tash over the edge, but the girls know my sense of humour and I think they used it as an excuse to get rid of me.

All I can do now is take the high road and wish them every success in the world.

# 18

# Plastic Fantastic?

I'm no stranger to surgery. What can I say? I can't resist a cheeky freebie and in this business you get offered procedures left, right and centre and it's so hard to say no. Especially when you're not fully confident in the way you look.

You see, I've had issues with my body since my first divorce. I know I was a little firecracker when I was young, I had the blonde hair, the big boobs. I was alright looking, me! But after Brian left, I went on the heartbreak diet. I lost a lot of weight and my boobs ended up like spaniel ears. It was hard watching him move on with someone so goddamn perfect like Delta Goodrem (his next girlfriend) – even I would've left me for her!

But it made me so self conscious of my looks and body. She hasn't had any children, I had! I started picking apart every blemish and curve and wondering if that was why he'd left me. Was it because I'd had kids and my body had changed?

After we split up I started to carve out a decent career for myself in the media – I was a tabloid's dream, but with that came this horrible body shaming culture that exists to this day. And that's when my body issues got really, really bad.

And as I've gotten older, it hasn't stopped. If anything, going into your forties, the expectation on you just gets bigger and bigger. Women don't seem to be allowed to grow old gracefully!

That said, it's not always been about vanity for me.

My breasts have always been big, but I opted to have a boob job back in 2004, something I reversed four years later when I had Max and Heidi.

And from then I've had a couple of other procedures, including a lift in 2019.

The fact of the matter is, my boobs are so, so heavy that I've had terrible problems with my back as a result. The aches and pains have been unreal, to the point where I could barely move at one point. The pain would make me physically sick.

So I made the decision to have a boob reduction in 2021, going from an F cup to a small D, in an effort to try and alleviate some of the agony.

The operation happened to coincide with a fun little show I did called Trash Monsters. I knew the filming schedule would interfere with my recovery, but, me being me, I put it to the back of my mind and figured I'd grit my teeth and get through it. After all, I hate turning down work, especially decent TV shows that help pay the bills.

So, just a few days before filming began I had my boob reduction, which was documented for Steph's Packed Lunch.

I had a few days in a hotel to recover, but it never gets any easier, these nips and tucks. And in hindsight, I should've rested more. But, as I say, I was contracted to do Trash Monsters a week later and there was no way I was backing out.

For those of you who missed it (how very dare you – catch it on YouTube or the All 4 app, it must be still doing the rounds!) the premise of the show sees a group of celebrities wear their own rubbish. Two weeks worth of your household trash is made into a suit that you wear around, in an effort to highlight waste and whatnot. It's a silly idea really, but I was up for it. I love being on TV, I love getting myself out there and trying new things, plus I got to work with Jodie Kidd, John Barnes and John Richardson, who I think are all brilliant.

So anyway, there I am just a few days after surgery and they put that suit of rubbish on me. Within hours, my face went bright red and I thought I was about to pass out. I had to lie down! It was seriously one of the most uncomfortable experiences of my life. Remember I'd only just had my chest cut open a few days before.

But my discomfort didn't end there, oh no.

Good old John Barnes, who I love to death by the way, saw me lying down, having a rest between takes on a sofa, and decided to jump on me. He didn't mean anything by it other than to be funny and playful and have a hug, which normally I would welcome with open arms and he obviously didn't realise about the surgery I'd had! But you can only imagine what a big man he is and oh my God, I thought I was going to break!

"Jesus, John what are you like!?" I squealed, as he let out that famous cheeky laugh of his. I had to laugh it off, although I did so through gritted teeth – which in hindsight sounded more like a muffled wail – because I was in so much pain.

Believe me, wearing your own rubbish is uncomfortable enough as it is, but add some plastic surgery into the mix, a giant John Barnes and a bear hug – and bloody hell!

# Plastic Fantastic?

The problem is, people don't have much empathy for the pain you go through when you have cosmetic procedures, but a boob job is a big deal and I should never have had it done before doing the show. It was too close together and in hindsight that was my mistake.

But me being me, as fucked up in the head as I am, I didn't stop there. Oh no, just days after I finished filming the show, I went straight back under the knife again, while at the same time still unpacking from my latest move up north.

This time I thought I'd go for a cheeky little tummy tuck – something I've not revealed publicly until now.

It wasn't needed and it wasn't necessary, but it was free. I need to stick to goodie bags, me. They're a lot less painful.

Turns out having a tummy tuck while moving house isn't the best idea. The aftermath of the surgery was a nightmare. I should've listened to my doctor – and my body – and rested up rather than turn myself into a removal van man. I was taking control of everything when it came to the move. I can't just sit back and let other people organise my house!

Before long my legs swelled up like balloons. I was in a bad way. I thought it was pockets of fat building up in my limbs, but it's actually excess fluid under my skin, all there as a result of my failure to take care of myself properly. Even now, because I didn't listen to the doctor, my stomach swells up and I look six months pregnant. I didn't give myself the proper aftercare I needed because I'm so bloody impatient!

Meanwhile, my boob job hadn't really worked out as I'd hoped either. They were still huge.

I was so, so unhappy with them. I was supposed to be getting smaller, pert boobs that wouldn't leave me crippled in pain. But if anything, they swelled up even more. I was starting to look like Quasimodo.

My whole body was in agony. My legs permanently resembled tree trunks – and still do to this day – and no amount of exercise seems to change that. It's like my body changed shape for the worse.

It certainly didn't help that my diet had gone to pot in lockdown and seeing my body become so deformed just made me so down. I basically gave up when it came to healthy eating.

I was getting loads of work in – which was amazing – but when I did have a day off I'd sit and eat shit. So even after the tummy tuck, designed to get me slim, I was still not being sensible with my nutrition. Believe it or not, after a boob reduction and a tummy tuck I ended up weighing MORE afterwards. Was it water retention? Swelling? My bad diet? Who knows but it was NOT worth it.

It's my own fault really. I know exactly what my issue is: I don't stop. I've always been a grafter, always earned my own money and always put food on the table for my kids. And there was no question, despite having major surgery just days before, that I wasn't going to do Trash Monsters.

During the pandemic I was even looking for jobs in the healthcare sector, just to have something to do and to make sure I could provide for my family.

So doing the show was something I would always have gone through with. I was hired, I was getting paid, why would I ever cancel? Regardless of how I was feeling?

Still, those surgeries left me with so many bloody ailments.

You can see when I was on Coach Trip, when I was filming

until 6am, I was in agony. Just watch it back and tell me you can't see me wince at certain points.

I ended up living with the pain constantly. It affected my life to the point where it was ruling it. I was washing DJ's hair in the bath and I had to stop. I physically couldn't do it anymore. Just washing my little girl's hair! How ridiculous is that!?

I hated my body, the way I felt like it was failing me. I hated the pain. And I hated the way I looked. Hate, hate, hate.

And, even though I've since had the surgery to try and rectify the damage, including another successful boob reduction, psychologically that mentality remains. Maybe it'll never go. After all I've been sliced and diced so much I need an instruction manual on how to put me back together!

As I mentioned, I do think my age is playing a massive part in my insecurities, what with being with a man who's so much younger than me.

Believe it or not people, it's difficult going out with a gorgeous toyboy! And there's absolutely no problem on Ryan's part, he genuinely makes me feel secure and never comments on my body – they're all issues of my own.

I always feel so aware of my body. There was a point at the beginning of 2022 when I couldn't actually look at myself in the mirror. The size of me, I looked like an actual beast. And I know they're strong words and if people look to me as some sort of 'showbiz role model' (please don't), then they probably think I'm irresponsible for saying that. Women should love themselves no matter what and all that. But it's easier said than done.

Like most women, I've had a difficult relationship with food for as long as I can remember. Not anorexia or bulimia, or anything like that, it's more the mistreatment of my body due to overeating. I've never stuck my fingers down my throat, or starved myself, I eat the wrong food for emotional reasons.

As I eat I think horrible things about myself. And it's always junk food. It's something even now I can't shake, which is why on Trash Monsters you saw so many takeaway packets in my rubbish.

You see, the biggest battle I have is with myself. It's something I really struggle with. I know I'm feeling down when my weight goes up. I'll wake up at 2am and binge on chocolate. I won't throw up or anything like that, I'll just wolf down the chocolate until my stomach physically can't take anymore. And it's always in the middle of the night.

On the worst nights you'll find piles and piles of chocolate and sweet wrappers on the floor next to my bed the following morning.

I need to keep a routine, you see. If something goes wrong in my day, just one thing can mess everything up. A lot of it is to do with my bipolar. It's something I can't control, but if something messes up my routine I can really get low. And then I'll binge on junk food.

Also – and this is probably where people will think I've gone mad – chocolate seems to stimulate really lovely, realistic dreams for me. And when I wake in the night I'm tempted to eat more of the stuff just to get back into those good dreams and escape reality a bit longer.

People will read this and think I need sectioning!

Since I moved back up north, keeping a routine going has been hard, what with the problems I've had since surgery. The fact it made my body worse angered me, which didn't help my mental state one bit and only increased my comfort eating. It's a dangerous cycle. I know I do have to watch my health.

*****

Obviously the boob job and tummy tuck have been negative experiences for me, but it doesn't put me off surgery.

I've been offered a free chin tuck, a hair transplant, all sorts! And to be honest if it's free, I'll take it. I go to a fantastic doctor, Dr Nyla Raja, at her Alderley Edge branch for my face, she does an incredible non-surgical facelift that keeps me looking fresh, so big shout out to her and her team. And I wouldn't stop at my face.

I had a bald patch in my head and I know for a fact it was because of all the hair extensions and stuff I had to wear for photoshoots (What can I say? I just love looking young!) But it's really taken a toll on my scalp, so I'm bang up for a transplant to sort that out too.

Like I said, I hate when people try to hold me up as some sort of role model because I'm in the public eye. I'm in my forties, I've had five kids, I've got every right to have whatever I want nipped and tucked.

If you break a nose and you get it fixed, no one says anything then! Or if you have sticking out ears and you pin them back – so what?! When a man gets a hair transplant, no one says a word, do they? But as a woman, if I decide I want that, I'll be slated to high heaven.

'Oh you're plastic, oh you're fake!' Well you know what? If surgery helps me with my confidence, then what on earth is the problem I ask you?

And besides, I do what I do mainly to rectify problems I have. It's not like I'm getting duck lips or fillers in my cheeks for the sake of it, which so many youngsters do nowadays. And that's something that does worry me about my daughters.

These influencers and reality stars, they're all starting to look the same. And I know it affects my girls too. Lilly's already asked me before what I think of her having a boob job. I've told her to wait until she's 21 and then make a decision, but ultimately she decided against it, she's happy with who she is. And so she should be, what I wouldn't give to have her figure!

I told her, "Lilly, do you know how much I'd love to wear a vest with no bra?! To walk around without back pain?"

But equally I can't tell her not to do stuff with her body, after what I've done to myself. I've had so many nips and tucks over the years, it would be so hypocritical of me to tell my kids they can't have something done.

To be honest I don't think Lilly's bothered, but I know my Heidi has terrible insecurities that really frighten me.

She's very self-obsessed. I never went through that with my older girls, because when they were Heidi's age Instagram and filters and TikTok and God knows what just wasn't a thing. You go on Instagram now and these thirteen year-olds look 21.

I remember the Halloween party we had when Heidi was 14, where she wanted to dress like a sexy school girl. And to me that's scary. She's still an 'actual' school girl! Molly and Lilly never went through that. But even though there's only four years between Heidi and Lilly, they're a whole generation apart.

Honestly, people think when you have five kids you know it all – well you don't! I'm learning something new every day. I did a live Instagram once, a video that goes out into the world immediately, and Heidi was in it. Of course to me she looked absolutely beautiful, but Heidi being Heidi, she found fault. And on this occasion she didn't like her arms. She was heartbroken and made me delete the footage entirely. That level of unnecessary insecurity is something that frightens me about her generation. All she ever says to me when we're out and about is, "Mum, isn't that girl pretty?" or, "She's famous because she's pretty".

It's like she can't see what I see.

"Heidi you're beautiful," I told her during one such conversation.

It was as if she didn't hear me.

"Why can't I look like you and Lilly?" she asked.

"Oh darling, we have our own insecurities as well you know," I told her. "And I get it."

I can see Heidi going down the route of getting fillers, because that's all she sees on Instagram. I know I've had it done, but not to the point where I look like a duck or a different person entirely. But for some reason, that's the look her generation wants to have! Plus, I'm not doing it because of what I see online.

I still look like me. It's just there's no wrinkles. And I think at my age it's acceptable to get a tweak here and there. But Heidi's a teenager!

It's something I'll have to keep an eye on, as, from a mother's point of view, of course I don't want her to change herself. But as someone who's been under the knife a fair bit, I suppose I'm not in any position to tell her that.

I just hope it's something she grows out of, or maybe, in an ideal world, society will come full circle and we'll stop fixating on looks over talent.

# 19

# Onwards And Upwards

All my life I've been drawn to controlling men. It must stem from my daddy issues but even when it comes to picking the people that work for me, I can't seem to get it right.

During the George days, when things were really bad, my then manager, Paul, was always there for me. He stood by me knowing what George was like. He'd give in to George's demands for money to save me from getting a good hiding, like the time he stuck £1500 in my bank account because George had his hands around my neck threatening to kill me if he didn't get the cash.

In a lot of ways I'm grateful that Paul had my back during those terrible times. But really, it was only when we parted ways and I started to get clarity over everything that had happened, that I started to question our business relationship.

I couldn't understand why, after George and I split, I wasn't getting work. Soon after I got together with Ryan, someone who's completely savvy when it comes to money and business, he sat me down one day and asked some unusual questions.

"Do you ever see any contracts and things like that?" he asked.

"No, my manager deals with it all," I replied, not really thinking much of it.

But weirdly, it stuck in my mind after and I sent Paul an email asking if I should start approving some contracts, based on what Ryan had asked.

"Don't trust Ryan," came the unexpected reply.

Remember Paul had never met Ryan at this point, but my attitude was already changing and the fact I was asking certain questions had obviously rattled him a bit.

I chose to ignore him and put it down to protectiveness on Paul's part. After all, with everything he'd witnessed with George, it was understandable why he wouldn't trust a new man in my life. Especially one that was questioning my finances.

But Ryan was so inspiring to me. He was so ambitious and he'd get excited over the smallest of opportunities. He thought outside the box and being around him reminded me how like that I was too.

I got to thinking.

When I was single, companies would send me clothes to post on Instagram. So I'd share a picture of me wearing the outfit and, lo and behold, their sales would go up. And it suddenly hit me. Why on earth wasn't I doing this myself? Why shouldn't I set up my own clothing company and make the money myself?

I did all the research, sorted all the figures, everything necessary to get a business like that started. And I rang Paul to tell him about it. I wanted to put everything forward to him as I trusted him.

"Sorry Kerry," he said once I'd outlined what I wanted to do.

"I don't see any of this happening. It's not the right move for you."

Oh. That was that, then.

By this point I'd been researching a few different ideas, so I changed tack.

"Ok, well what about a YouTube channel? Or a book?"

"No, no to both."

My confidence sank to the floor. Something wasn't right. Why was he so down on my ideas? Influencers all over the internet were doing stuff like this, and there was me, who'd been in the industry for years, who was still selling magazine covers, and he didn't think people would be interested?! I was desperate for work as well, to pay the next bill, and I had thoughts on how I could go about it.

I had to have it out with him and find out what on earth was going on in his head.

We met in McDonald's a few days later.

"Why am I not getting any work?" I asked, outright. "I have so many ideas about TV work in the future. You know there's a new series of SAS? And Celebs On the Farm? I'd be perfect! Have you put me forward?"

Paul looked me in the eye. "Yes I have, and they don't want you," he said.

"What do you mean they don't want me? If I'm doing something wrong, tell me so I can fix it."

He just stared at me. "People think you're unreliable," he said. "They think you're all over the place because you talk too much about your mental health and about God. It's off-putting."

My heart sank. I couldn't get my head around it. After George died I was open about my struggles and what I'd been through,

I'd revealed I was back on antidepressants and as a result I'd got so much support from people. Times were changing and the public were becoming so much more receptive to conversations about mental health.

"So because I was open and honest about what happened to me when my baby's daddy died, I'm being blacklisted?" I was so confused. "Paul, I could've gone off the rails. I could've gone down the drugs route again. Instead I went to my doctor and I did it the right way. And you're saying because of that people won't work with me?! Do I need to go off the rails again to get work?!"

He told me I needed to rein it in a bit. I was absolutely furious.

"Who told you all this, Paul? Where did you get this from?"

"A close source," he said.

"Who's the bloody 'source'?" I asked, getting irate. "Ketchup?!"

"It was actually someone at a national magazine," he said.

I couldn't believe what I was hearing. Everything and anything I wanted to do he threw back at me, because apparently some random person at a mag had told him I was unreliable.

My stomach turned in that moment because I felt like he'd let me down. It seemed like he hadn't fought for me. I knew he had other, bigger clients to deal with and it just appeared to me as if he'd lost all interest in even promoting me.

Looking back, my self-esteem was on the floor working with Paul at that time and I soon realised that getting away from him was the best option for me. It was hard because for so long he'd been there for me on an emotional level, looking after me when George was at his worst. But the time had come for a fresh start with new management who I felt would give me the support I deserved and, in a way, I'm grateful it played out the way it did.

Finding the strength to leave my management and go it alone was hard. I was so drained from the previous decade with George, and Paul's words about me being "off-putting" were so stinging I found it hard to even contemplate moving on. I just wanted to give up at that moment. How could I possibly leave Paul anyway? He had control of most of my cash and would supplement me with pocket money from the small amount of projects I did manage to get. I felt trapped again at the hands of a man, even if only in a business sense.

But with the support of Ryan, who is so savvy, I knew I could get free. Although terrified that I was financially tied down to Paul, there had to come a point in my life where I stood on my own two feet. I've always been a grafter and I should've known from the start I could make it on my own.

Surely it can't be *that* difficult to go from nothing to a millionaire, back to bankruptcy and back to a millionaire again in one lifetime?

I started to realise that if anyone could do it, I could.

I prayed. I said my affirmations, pulled my socks up, got a decent accountant who was able to pick apart who owed what to who, and started to work bloody hard. I wanted to invest in myself. Not stocks and shares, but in me. I lifted the phone and started calling people myself. TV companies and programmes listened as I pitched myself and the offers started flooding in – and that told me that I had definitely made the right decision.

I left Paul soon after that meeting in McDonald's. What a way to bow out, after everything we'd been through, sitting there, realising in my heart we were essentially breaking up, while people munched on quarter pounders and fries around us.

The weird thing is, since I parted ways with him, every single one of the ideas I put forward to him – the ones he shot down without even a conversation – I made happen on my own.

I ended up winning Celebs on the Farm. SAS had me on and both me and the show made headlines around the country. I'm a regular on the excellent Steph's Packed Lunch on Channel 4. Me and Lilly did Celebrity Ghost Trip, which we won and had the most amazing time filming. It's the first time I've done a show with one of my daughters and we had a blast. I also took part in Celebrity Cooking School, which was another amazing experience. There were even talks about a possible podcast with the BBC!

I started my own clothing range, Kerry's Boutique, I got involved with Thrillz, which is a great site where people can buy personalised video messages from me. I set up a YouTube channel which now gets thousands of subscribers and viewers just watching me and the family going about our daily lives. Ryan and I have created a dating app called Marnii, which continues to go from strength to strength, and we've also launched an awesome fitness site called M-Fit in which Ryan is able to put his skills as a businessman and personal trainer to good use.

Don't you think it's mad that I made all those projects happen barely a year after I was told, in no uncertain terms, that "nobody wants to work with me"?

When Paul realised I was making all this happen he told me I was to share all my earnings with him. "I own you," he said.

It was the last straw for me.

No one owns me.

After George, at least I had the wisdom to know that much. I haven't spoken to Paul since – something which suits both of us just fine – but my dealings with him did make me realise once again that the only person you can, and should, rely on is yourself. It was my sheer hard work that made it all happen, not my manager's, or anyone else. Although, obviously shout out to Ryan for being an amazing partner and the absolute inspiration in helping me get back on my feet.

*****

I've done so many wonderful things that have seen me get my profile and my finances back to where they once were. Although none have been as effective, or indeed as controversial, as my decision to sign up to OnlyFans, an adult website that allows people to pay money to see whatever I allow them to see.

The idea to do it raised a few eyebrows at first, but the way I see it? What's the difference in flogging some topless bikini pics to a pap for the papers to splash on, when I can control the images myself? If people want to pay to see pics of my boobs, who am I to say no? Seems like a no brainer to me!

When I first decided to join the site I was still with Paul, but when I asked him what he thought he simply replied, "I just don't think you'd do well on something like that. I can't really imagine people will pay for that sort of thing."

Charming.

I decided to do it anyway, as I saw the potential to make a lot of money and I could see other celebs making a killing on it, their reputations fully intact.

When Paul knew I was serious about going ahead with joining the site, he wanted to take control of the whole thing, to set up the account in his name and everything. He claimed he would be able to get a better discount on the 20 per cent that

OnlyFans take, but that wasn't the case because I had become good friends with the owner of the site, so I knew what was what. My instinct told me to carry on setting up my profile alone, which is what I did.

Seriously, the relief when the money started coming in! I knew that I could start paying my way and also get rid of any 'debt' I had to Paul. According to him I owed him for my car rental and all sorts but once an accountant had been through everything with a fine-tooth comb, they said I didn't actually owe him anything at all.

Suddenly I was making good cash again. Enough for us to move into a larger house, back up north.

Enough for me to breathe a sigh of relief that I could get my kids back into private education, and sort out their school uniforms on my own without help from anyone else.

It seems it really does pay to get your kit off!

When I started on OnlyFans I was in great shape, proud of my body and feeling good about myself. Of course that changed after surgery, but I stuck on a smile, acted confident and people bought it.

In fact, I was soon one of the highest earners on the site. People would pay to see my boobs and would send me gorgeous sexy outfits for me to wear in photos just for them. I even had people with foot fetishes wanting to see pics of my feet. I'm sorry, but in my mind, taking a picture of your feet is easy money and if guys wanted to pay me to do that, who was I to argue?

The first photos I took were a collaborative effort between me, Ryan and Molly and dead funny, looking back. It was no different to going to a fashion shoot! I was in my knickers and bra, Ryan was putting the oil on and Molly would be doing the lighting while I stood there like a zombie not wanting to get baby oil on my walls. There was nothing shameful about it, if anything, it was fun and the fact we were open about what I was doing just meant no one was embarrassed or upset by it.

In fact, I'd sat the kids down a few weeks previously and asked them what they thought of me doing it. It's important to me that I'm transparent with the children when it comes to things like this. They were all totally fine with it, and when they saw the money come in they were bloody thrilled!

It is crazy how much I earn now and the community is like no other. As I've said, I do have issues with my body, but with OnlyFans, that's all out of the window, so long as you pretend to be confident. You can be any shape or size and people love you for that. There's no filter. It's not like in the magazines where you've got to look a certain way or where they airbrush any stretch marks and cellulite out. It's real life and people do pay to see it!

I was – and continue to be – a huge success on the site. I have loyal followers and apparently there's a few celebs who keep an eye on me too.

Case in point: I met this ex-footballer a while ago and I've worked with him a few times on and off, for charity matches and whatnot over the years. Now, I won't name him but I can assure you he's a household name.

Anyway, I've often enjoyed a bit of banter with him, he makes me laugh, he's a funny guy! But the last time I saw him, which was quite recently, I sensed there was something a bit 'off' with him. He was making little digs to me, insinuating things that I wasn't massively comfortable with, about my body, my sex life, etc. So I had to call him out on it. There was no way I could let it go because I felt like he was taking the mick. I couldn't bear it!

In my head, based on some of the stuff he was coming out with, I believed he was insinuating I'd slept with one of his old teammates back in the day, which I hadn't. We'll call said teammate Terry for now.

"Listen you, what's the story?" I asked Mr Household Name. "What's with the digs? It feels a bit demeaning. I know you think I slept with Terry, but I didn't!"

He looked taken aback. "That didn't even cross my mind," he said, and he seemed genuine.

I let it go. I was confused but maybe I was being overly sensitive and I'd been reading it all wrong.

A few days later I was back in Mr H-N's company again.

The two of us were there, working, chatting when he piped up, "You could make a million quid this year, Kerry."

I laughed. "I already have love!"

He looked at me wide eyed. "How?"

"OnlyFans," I said. He acted like he didn't have a clue what OnlyFans was, so I explained the premise to him.

"I get my kit off and people pay to see it, who am I to argue with that?' I winked.

He looked intrigued but then a smirk quickly spread across his face.

"It's a shame, I've never seen that shower scene on OnlyFans," he said, almost laughing.

I stopped in my tracks. What on earth was he rambling on about? I'd never mentioned anything about a shower scene. Yes, I've done one – but I hadn't told him about it!

There was a glint in his eye.

"Yeah, I've never cleaned my mobile phone screen off after watching you," he carried on, sarcasm dripping from his voice.

Oh bloody hell. I think we all know what the insinuation here was.

Turns out this household name, a family man in fact, subscribes to my OnlyFans, and had all along, hence the dirty little digs, and he'd just admitted he'd masturbated to my videos.

I didn't even know what to say about it. What do you say to that?!

But he didn't stop there. He went on to tell me there's "a group of us that love OnlyFans".

I laughed it off, because what else could I do? The guy's using a service I willingly provide! But I'd never ever been told that before. Yes, men send messages, dick pics and the like, but to brazenly tell me to my face they've had an orgasm all over their mobile phone while watching a video of me in the shower?! That was new territory.

Once I'd left this famous face I got in my car and my jaw just fell to the floor. I rang Ryan and told him everything straight away. I was mortified! But it goes to show that the site is more widely used than even I imagined.

*****

I'm smart enough to know my own worth when it comes to OnlyFans. That money I'm making bought me a new Lamborghini. It's ensured my kids can stay in private education. So who's having the last laugh now?

I started up my own dating app, a fitness app, a clothing brand and OnlyFans is the thing I make the most from. So, good luck to anyone who gives it a go, there's enough room in the world for us all to whip our kits off if that's what people want to pay to see.

If I'm not worried or upset about it, there's no reason anyone else should be.

My body, my life, my rules.

## 20

# Fourth Time Lucky

August 2020 and the world was still stuck in a vicious cycle of lockdowns. Even as they started to ease up and people gradually began to meet up again, the threat of Covid was everywhere. It felt like the country was trapped in a never-ending bubble of fear and anxiety.

That's why it feels almost wrong to say at this point in my private and professional life I was back at the top of my game and – despite the world outside my door – I was happier than ever.

I was making a killing on OnlyFans, I'd dumped my bad business associates and suddenly I was more in demand than ever. Which means, most importantly, the money was coming in, allowing me to feed my kids comfortably. It's funny what happens when you clear out the negativity from your life. Good things.

And the best thing ever was just around the corner.

As is obvious by now, marriage has never been my forte. I've always looked at relationships as something I need, rather than something I want. It all stems from childhood abandonment and the feeling of craving love and stability above all else. Of course, the neediness has meant I've ended up with three husbands who were no good for me.

After George I was put off marriage for good. How could I possibly go through that again?! Surely I'd learnt my lesson that no man is worth sacrificing everything for.

But – and I know you'll roll your eyes at this as you've heard me say it a thousand times before, but it's true – Ryan was different.

Ryan is the first man I've ever been with who I don't *need*. And that's not me putting him down, that's just a fact. I don't need him – but I want him. And that's a wonderful, healthy place to be at in a relationship.

I'm financially independent, I have my kids and yet here is this man that I want to share all that with. Who I have built that with, who doesn't need anything from me in return.

I can honestly say with my hand on my heart that everything about my relationship with Ryan feels different – in a weird way! – because for the first time in my life I'm settled and free of drama. I know he'll never leave me, and I'll never leave him. We have created a life for ourselves that's so successful and comfortable that tearing it apart just wouldn't be an option.

It was an unsettling feeling at first, being with a man who put me before anything. I've never had a man treat me so well with such genuine good intentions and it's something that's taken me a long time to get used to. But once I was used to it, I knew I was stuck with him for good – and I wouldn't have it any other way.

Ryan popped the question one gorgeous night in August, with a £16k ring from the Queen's jeweller, no less.

We were on holiday in Spain, where I was celebrating my 40th early. My birthday's actually in September but due to the travel rules at the time I knew I'd be quarantined when I got back, so we used Spain as an excuse to have a big celebration and make it special.

The night of the party everyone I wanted to be there was there, and that included all the kids. We had DJs, a private chef, the full works and it was turning into a cracking night. I let my hair down and enjoyed a few glasses of Prosecco to fully make the most of turning 40. Even now I wonder how I've made it so far. It felt like a real milestone.

Anyway, the party was in full swing, and I was downstairs, drinking away, when Max came down, dead casual, to tell me Ryan needed me upstairs, something about an email I needed to look at. Ryan has since said he wanted the proposal itself to be private, so I'm guessing that was his ruse. A good one it was, and Max did so well.

I made it upstairs and that's when I saw the rose petals all over the bed and the floor – and I knew straight away what was about to happen.

Ryan took my hand and led me onto the balcony.

"You know I love you, right?" he asked me.

My heart was jumping out of my chest and I could barely speak. I could only nod.

"Will you marry me?"

In an instant all my fears about a fourth marriage melted away. Partly when I saw the size of the ring! I joke of course – he could've given me a piece of metal from Argos and I would've still said yes. But there was something about that moment. The Spanish setting, having my family there with me, the romance of it all, it was beautiful and I just knew it was right. There was no hysteria, no crying, no shrieking, it was all very calm and relaxed and different to any of my other proposals. It was the best one yet – and that's saying something considering I've been proposed to a lot! I was actually in bed by 9pm that night and the party went on without me. We didn't go wild into the night, I just felt very content and at peace. I guess that's how relationships *should* feel.

All the kids were as thrilled as I was. They'd been part of the surprise all along – I was wondering why they were all wearing flowers in their hair for the occasion! And then of course I realised. Ryan had kept them in the loop from the beginning, right down to asking their thoughts on the ring.

He later revealed what they'd said in a magazine interview.

He recalled, 'I'd rang Molly and Lilly to tell them what I had planned and I sent them both a picture of the ring. Lilly loved it, she sent me back a load of 'love eyes' emojis. Molly took a while to reply, she's a bit more protective of her mum, but we get on so well that once I spoke to her she was fully on board. I also phoned Kerry's mum Sue, to let her know what I was planning. She was in tears on the phone when I told her! It was a total green light to go from her.'

He was right, Mum was delighted. I got straight on the phone to her when we got engaged as she wasn't at the party. She won't get on a plane to go anywhere. Not even my 40th.

"Mum, I'm getting married… again," I said, expecting her to sigh down the phone.

Instead she was thrilled. So much so she was crying her eyes out, just as she had done with Ryan when he initially told her of his plan.

"This is the first time I haven't got the jelly belly, where I was thinking, 'Please don't do this, Kerry'", she sobbed. "It's the first time I know for a fact you're not making a mistake."

I surprised myself by how emotional I felt to hear her say that. I started to get a bit choked up.

"Ryan's the best person you could've ever met," she said.

Well, you can't argue with that.

I said at the time that I really wanted to go to Vegas and get married, but in hindsight I was running away with myself a bit. I've not had the Covid vaccine – more on that later – and it means that travel to the US might well be tricky as a result.

So we've abandoned that idea for now. We're still trying to work out what we want and when we want to do it but one thing's for sure, I'm not in a huge hurry. We're very happy as we are and super busy, so it's not something we feel we need to rush.

There's also the tricky aspect of me still being legally married to George. As a widow I know I'm free to marry again but there are some legalities that need to be dealt with, so that's on the to-do list as well.

When I think back over Ryan's proposal, and indeed the years since I met him, it's clear what an amazing, positive influence he's been on me. We're polar opposites, a bit like chalk and cheese and we argue like cat and dog but it works.

I used to say to him, "Did you ever think you'd be engaged to somebody who's eight years older, divorced twice, widowed, bankrupt twice, an ex-coke addict, with five children by three different dads?"

And he'd always put my mind at ease and tell me how happy our little blended family made him.

He'd joke, "Written down on paper it sounds a lot, but day to day, the reality is I'm happy and we're happy as a family."

But I know there's one thing that is missing for Ryan – and that's a baby of his own.

He's an incredible dad to my kids, and luckily he's been in DJ's life now since she was very small, so I know she sees him as a father figure. So do Max and Heidi. And I know Molly and Lilly adore him as well.

And that's why I feel so guilty – but my heart tells me I won't be able to give him that biological child he craves. Ryan's so laid back, he's very much 'what will be will be', but I know him and I know he'd love to be a dad to his own.

But after DJ's birth and the trauma that surrounded it, I just don't think I could go through it again. Add to that the fact I'm now in my forties and it feels somehow selfish to bring another baby into the world.

I already have such terrible anxiety about the fact I won't have as much time with DJ as I will the others, so how could I justify having another baby right now?

I just don't want to put my body or my mind through it.

We've discussed other options, potentially surrogacy and egg donors, but the fact remains – once the baby is here, we'll still be raising it with five other children and our dogs, as well as juggling our business empire. I don't want to have to sacrifice anything now that we've worked so hard for it.

And remember, before I was having babies because it was a way to keep the men. The men I married wanted kids and I was keen to deliver, in order to keep the relationship together. But I don't have those same insecurities with Ryan. I know we don't need a baby of our own to keep us together.

For a long time I've been going back and forth on the decision and as I write this, I can safely say there will be no more children for me.

I'm so blessed and grateful for the little rugrats I have and I don't need to add to that. Been there, done that!

I think it's something Ryan has accepted – he's as ambitious as I am and I'm sure that right now his desire to keep the businesses going outweighs his need for a baby of his own.

Who knows, that might all change – by the time you read this I could be wandering about pregnant again, but I really don't see it happening.

I want to give Ryan everything he wants, much in the same way he's done for me, but he understands that another baby is a bridge too far. I was so traumatised after having DJ that the thought of putting myself through that again – potentially dying – for something I don't really want and doing it only for a man – well, it's not who I am anymore.

In my pre-George mindset that's exactly what I would've done to make someone like Ryan stay with me, but I know he's not going anywhere – baby or not.

# 21

# Not So Happy Holidays

Fast forward 18 months or so and it was just before Christmas 2021. The end of another particularly terrible year for everyone, although personally and professionally I had smashed it, so I wasn't complaining.

That said, for some reason, at this point my anxiety was at an all-time high. I can't even explain it, I just had this ominous feeling I couldn't shift. And that in itself scared me, as throughout my life, if I feel like something bad's about to happen, a premonition if you will, it usually does. It's like I'm psychic or something.

I was performing in panto in Oldham, alongside Bruce Jones of Coronation Street fame and things were going fine but I just couldn't work out what was going on in my head. I just wasn't myself. Was it the panto or the pandemic? Or something else?

I'm not one to manifest negativity, I do always try and look on the bright side of things, but perhaps in this case I did?

I wasn't put up in the best hotel for panto – and that's not me being a snob, it genuinely wasn't a nice place to stay. Lots of piss-heads about. DJ even asked if we could sleep in the car, rather than stay there. I didn't like it at all.

One night I couldn't sleep, I wasn't comfortable and I ended up staying up watching a show about robberies, called Thick as Thieves. The next day I remember texting Ryan, because my anxiety was through the roof.

'I need you here, I don't know what's wrong with me,' I said desperately via Whatsapp. 'Something just doesn't feel right.'

Whatever it was, I believe now it was a premonition of what was to come: a Christmas blighted by Covid, stress, arguments and a crime that threatened to tear my family apart.

*****

As a little treat one crisp winter morning I took Max and DJ shopping to a retail park in Oldham, in between panto performances.

We had a lovely day, eating Nando's and visiting the toy shops. The kids were in their element. In fact it was such a successful trip I ended up loading up my car with toys for Christmas, easily £300's worth. Anyway, we got back to the hotel I was staying at but I forgot to unload the toys from the boot to give to Ryan for when he came to pick Max up. That proved to be a fatal error, the first of a couple on my part.

The next day I was with Heidi and DJ, we were heading back to the same retail park for some more shopping – it was the lead up to Christmas after all, so there was still lots to do.

We parked up in an open car park. I had my purse in my pocket, so I decided to leave my bag in the car. Now, of course, in hindsight that was a stupid mistake, but even though the area wasn't great, I didn't think for a second anything would happen. I should've paid attention to Heidi who was warning me, "Mum, there's two iPads in there – you'd be silly not to bring it with you."

Oh how I wished I'd listened to her.

After shopping I headed back to the car and as I approached it, I noticed the brake light come on. And from then, everything seemed to happen in slow motion. I'm watching goggle-eyed as the car starts up. I start thinking, 'Has Ryan come to pick the car up?' And then, as if I'm in a dream, I watch as the car drives away. "Ryan?!" But I know he's back at home.

I realised then it was being nicked. My instincts kicked in. I became frantic and started yelling. I broke away from the kids and started to run towards the car.

I could hear Heidi, although in my sheer fright her screaming sounded more like a mild whisper.

"Mum, come back! Be careful," she shouted, before dragging DJ back by her hood when the little one tried to follow me in a panic.

"Stop! Stop the car!" I screamed. "They're nicking me car."

Now of course by this point people were starting to stare, probably thinking, 'There goes Kerry Katona having another breakdown!'

It doesn't help that as I was running after the car I started to wet myself. I've had five kids, don't forget – I can't even jump without having a wee. But when you feel that dribble down your leg as you're racing across a car park in pursuit of a stolen vehicle as your kids scream behind you, well, it's not one of life's high points, let me tell you.

I took a few more steps and realised it was too much. I

couldn't run anymore at this point. And that was the moment when I suddenly snapped out of it and thought of the children. And I do feel guilty looking back, but I'd left them standing there in the middle of the car park on their own while I chased after my car.

I turned around and for a split second I couldn't see them. I felt sick to my stomach. My immediate thought was 'Oh my God they've been kidnapped. it's a ploy.' I thought I was going to have a heart attack on the spot.

Thank God I then spotted them in the crowd of people. From what I recall a very nice woman was trying to comfort a sobbing DJ, which, in my state of panic, just led me to scream at her 'get away from my child!'

I should apologise to that woman now while I have the chance. It wasn't my finest hour but I also wasn't totally convinced this wasn't all one big elaborate kidnap plot to extort money from me or something. When you're freaking out, nothing makes sense.

I must have looked a right state and even now I'm not sure what possessed me to leave the kids standing there while I attempted to leg it after the car like an incontinent Wonder Woman.

Witnesses who saw it happen said it was a gang, which seems to be the most likely explanation.

Everything must have happened in just seconds. But it felt like an eternity. And the best bit? It didn't stop there.

We were lucky to get a lift back home from some people I was working on the panto with, and in that time I must have been watched and followed. The fob for my front gate was in the stolen car. And whoever nicked it followed me home, waited a few days and then came back, opened the gate with the said fob and took Ryan's car as well.

As you can imagine this was both frightening and infuriating. Yes, I know they're just cars, but anyone who's been robbed will understand that feeling of being violated. Of having not just your personal possessions, but your lives and home, being infiltrated and taken against your will.

It was devastating.

The police couldn't find Ryan's car and still haven't, to this day. The gang had managed to dispose of his tracker and the number plates and installed fake ones quickly. A quarter of a million pounds worth of cars gone, just like that.

It was something that really hit us hard as a family. The fact someone came to the house frightened us all. I think it hurt Ryan's pride too that he felt he hadn't protected us, which is obviously crazy, but I have to understand his point of view. It led to a lot of arguments. We're talking about screaming matches here.

I was adamant I wanted a full blown security system in place, Ryan wanted to cut his losses and move back down south. We just couldn't agree on the best course of action but I knew in my heart leaving the house was the only option. It had to be. The place was now sullied. Cars get stolen all over the country and this was just bad luck at the hands of some very evil people, but still – something changed in me and I knew we had to get away.

Bear in mind I'd only been back living up north for six months when this all happened. It was a massive trigger because when I was living here before, with Mark Croft, I was held hostage at knifepoint by three masked men. I know I'm struggling, to this day, with PTSD and I associated living up here with that and so much more misery. So for this to happen, it feels like history repeating itself. It was an enormous trigger.

It also didn't help that Heidi and DJ seemed to be really affected by what they had witnessed.

DJ was oddly calm about it at first, but a few days later she started having these huge tantrums.

She was saying things no seven year-old should be saying and to be honest it frightened the hell out of me.

I'd walk into her room and she'd just suddenly kick off at me, screaming, "I hate myself, I want to kill myself." I'm crying my eyes out even thinking about it now.

I think – as well as the ongoing problems she has dealing with her dad's death – she witnessed something really scary in that car park. I was a mess and I feel terribly guilty because I'm scared it's badly affected her and Heidi.

I know I do let DJ get away with a lot – she still gets in bed with me and Ryan, she still goes everywhere with me – so perhaps I've mollycoddled her too much as a result of what she's been through. And maybe seeing me lose control in that car park has made her realise I'm not invincible either.

I also have to consider whether her tantrums are her reaction to mine and Ryan's frustration over everything that happened. We really were arguing a lot but in the end I got my way when I hired full-blown CCTV security for the house, before we ultimately left it. I even had men keep watch, otherwise there's no way I could've relaxed.

Ryan wasn't happy about it, he felt he should be enough to protect us, but of course I can't put it all on him. Just because he's the man of the house, it doesn't mean he can be – or should be! – responsible for keeping the place from being ransacked by scumbags.

To be honest the whole debacle triggered me. In the same way I ended up back in rehab after those masked men took me hostage.

They had knives. And knives reminded me of the time my stepdad Dave stabbed my mum and told her he was Freddy Krueger. I get triggered by these things. And I so wanted Ryan to understand that. Every rustle of the leaves, every twitch of the curtain in the wind, I'd jump up, my heart racing.

Security cameras and watchmen gave me just that, security. I felt for Ryan as I understood where he was coming from, but I couldn't have been happy if we didn't do something.

Of course it didn't help seeing trolls comment on the press reports saying it was an insurance job. I mean, come on! I don't need an insurance job with the amount of money I've now got coming in. And I worked so hard for that car. I'm entitled to nice things that I work hard for. Trolls will be trolls, but come on.

Anyway, I never saw the car again. The police didn't find it, despite reports that someone had crashed it. But to be honest, if it ever did show up I wouldn't step foot in it. No chance.

*****

While all this was going on in the aftermath of the robbery, we were stuck in isolation. Five of us managed to get Covid when the Omicron variant was doing the rounds. No one could come to us, we couldn't go anywhere and it was such a testing time. No wonder me and Ryan were at each other's throats and DJ was acting up so much.

On top of it all, I felt so, so ill. I've had Covid twice now and I tell you what, it knocks you for six.

It all started with Molly catching it, meaning she couldn't come back on the plane and spend Christmas with us. We were all so gutted. Molly was borderline hysterical, I think she felt guilty for getting it, but at that point I didn't know a single household that wasn't affected in some way. It felt like it was everywhere. And with little guidance from a useless government, it's no wonder people were falling ill left, right and centre.

So it was Molly first, then after the car madness Ryan got ill, swiftly followed by me.

Now I'm not vaccinated, and it's not something I shout or preach about. I don't want to be a role model for either side of the argument, it's a completely personal choice. Fair play to you if you want to get vaccinated, and good luck to you if you don't. I'm not 'anti vax' as I understand those sorts of connotations can be damaging, but it's something I personally have chosen to avoid.

I know people that have been double-jabbed and still died. Whereas I've had it twice and fought it off naturally both times.

The second time was bad – my vision went really terrible for a little bit – but not as bad as the first.

But I'm not having any jabs. Absolutely not. We're constantly being told how we have to be boosted – but how many times will that be?! It feels like it's endless.

It doesn't sit right with me and I don't want my children to have the vaccine either. It's a decision we've made as a family.

Mind you, Molly did decide to have all three jabs, which I wasn't best pleased about, and she *still* got Covid!

But there's no denying Covid took a lot out of me. In fact that whole period left me on the floor. I lost a lot of money through having to cancel panto, the cars were nicked, we couldn't go anywhere, we all felt rough – it's no wonder I had to drink to get through Christmas Day and Boxing Day – and that's not like me at all!

Even a few weeks later I could barely move when I went to get up. And being older and an ex-smoker I do think it got me good. But like I say, my immune system has still fought it every step of the way.

It wasn't just me, Ryan and DJ were out of sorts. All the stress and tension of it all became too much for poor Heidi, who managed to avoid Covid completely and ended up on a train back down south over the new year to spend it with her friends.

She tested negative and got out of the house as soon as she could. I think the rows and bickering and general atmosphere was too much.

It just goes to show those people not only stole a car, they really messed up a family, including the mental health of my kids who had to witness it. I get it's 'just a car' – I understand it's all material. But it's not even about that. The aftermath – the panic, the stress, the sadness, it's all part and parcel of it.

We couldn't even get it covered on insurance for a variety of reasons, which led to many more fights and stress with Ryan. It was endless and a really tough set of circumstances in a year that had given us so many other wonderful things.

Even though I totally get the impact it's had on my children, and I see how me and Ryan argued as a result, I still get that it's life, and these things happen.

But regardless of how anxious I got over it all, I knew I wasn't having a full blown breakdown, and I think that's shows how much I've grown as a person. I no longer anticipate rehab when I get low or anxious, I just acknowledge it's part of life and I have to deal with it.

With everything I've been through in my childhood, seeing a car being nicked should be almost normal for me, but it's not normal for my kids. They haven't experienced this sort of thing before and I don't want them to ever again. I also don't want them to worry that me and Ryan would ever fight like me and George did, because that would never happen.

So in light of it all, even now, I need to figure out the best ways to deal with things like this. Because, as the saying goes, shit happens.

# 22

# My World

After everything my kids have been through, it would be wrong of me not to dedicate at least one full chapter in the book solely to them, where I can really explain to everyone what a credit they are to me.

They've seen so much, and that's something I need to live with for the rest of my life, but I can honestly say with my hand on my heart that I'm dead proud of the people they've become.

Like all families we still have our issues and my children are very much a wonderful work in progress, but you won't find five more polite, respectful human beings.

As with any mother I worry about them all the time, of course. I hate Molly being so far away from home, living in Ireland, I wish she was back here with me full time, sitting on the couch and watching Netflix. One of the things I treasure most is our time together. And I'm so protective of her dreams. She wants to be an actress, which she's doing a degree in! And she's certainly got the talent for it. But Molly wants to do it on her own terms. She doesn't need me or her dad to get her on the map, she's doing it all on her own merit. She's a great singer as well, she definitely got her musical talent from her father, and she's a fantastic guitar player too, I just wish she had more of my upfront boldness, it's the one thing I could've passed on to her!

She was my absolute rock when George died, she came with me when I did press to talk about it, she held me as I cried and she stayed strong for the entire family. She's matured so much in recent years and I can honestly say she's my best friend. I want more than anything to see her talent realised, so she's gonna keep plugging away and I'll help endorse her where I can – even though she'd hate that!

In other words, if you're reading this, get on her Instagram and check out her tunes, she's got a gift. And I know she'll hate me for saying that because she's too shy for her own good.

Lilly's the one with a bit more of a showbiz mind. We've done a lot of TV and publicity work together now and it's clear that's where she thrives, in front of the camera. She's a natural. But she's not putting all her eggs in one basket and I think that's so important.

As someone who's seen what it's like to fall from grace, I know how essential it is to have a back-up career. During the pandemic I thought about stepping up and doing some work for the community because I couldn't bear to not graft at a time when there was no work coming in. Thankfully, that turned around pretty quickly, but that ethic never leaves me. And it's the same with Lilly.

When she's not being asked to be on Love Island (it was something she didn't feel comfortable doing, not when somewhere down the line she still dreams about being a lawyer), she was doing support work for the NHS, for mentally challenged younger adults. That is a huge responsibility and it proves just how driven she is.

It hasn't always been that way with her, though. In her terrible teens we definitely clashed. There were times when she had a really bad attitude, she wasn't necessarily in with the best crowd at school and I was really worried about her. To be fair, it was really tough for her after George died. It affected her a lot, she had a lot of resentment and hate and she would lash out at me as a result. The cross words we've had! We just weren't getting along. In that time her whole personality changed, so she went to stay with her dad for a bit.

The problem is, we are similar in so many ways that it was inevitable we'd butt heads. We're both strong willed and independent, and for a time I was really scared that I'd lose her. But isn't that every mother's fear when their little ones become teenagers? They don't need you as much anymore and they're desperate to follow their own path. And Lilly did for a while, I just had to hope she'd come through the difficult stage, which she did.

She's really come into her own, though I still worry about the choices!

We were in the car the other day and I asked her if she wanted kids. "Why on earth would I want kids?" she shot back, as if I'd just asked her if she wanted nuclear war.

I then asked if she wanted to get married.

"God no!" came her reply.

So there goes my dream of being a young grandmother out the window, unless Molly steps up! I was relying on grandkids! I would really love to be a young nan, I want to spend as much time as possible with my family, which is why I'm all about doing everything so young. But I guess the current generation has a different mindset.

I'm sure Lilly will change her mind as she gets older. Or at least I hope she does! I suppose she's grown up with lots of children around her, so she's probably over it. But you know what? That's fine, if it means she focuses on her career and goals, I won't be holding her back.

It's not only her career choices that impress me – Lilly's always been about doing what she wants to do. Even when it comes to religion.

She's a practising witch who's always been drawn to spells and crystals. She actually gave an interview about it to the press, where she discussed it and she was so eloquent and sounded so intelligent, I was dead proud.

"At the start of the first lockdown I was really struggling," she said. "Like everyone else I found it so hard and I was searching for something to make me feel better. I remember I went to the woods one day, and I actually got drawn down this path I'd never been down before. And there was this tree with a tiny fire burning by it. There was no one around, but there was a pagan symbol on the tree. It felt like a sign, so I went back and researched it and it took me down a Wicca rabbit hole. I realised it's such a beautiful religion, it's incredibly spiritual."

For an 18-year-old to speak like that, it's quite something! But I know she was on a mission to change people's perception of it. And after experiencing the horror of George when he started experimenting with the dark side, even I needed to be persuaded it was a good thing.

"It's so sad because it's so misunderstood," Lilly said in her interview. "There's such negative connotations around what witchcraft is. Like it's all 'evil women being burnt at the stake' and 'it's the devil's work'. But it's actually a wonderfully kind, good religion."

She does a lot of spells and uses crystals, mainly for her own personal growth, but also for health-related things, like just getting a peaceful night's sleep, for instance. She also does card readings and uses herbs. It's all pretty alien to me but I see it's calming for her, so however long it lasts, be it a phase or forever, I'm just happy she's happy.

*****

My little Heidi is the most gorgeous thing ever, but she remains a concern for me. You have to remember that when George died, it wasn't just DJ who lost her dad, it was the other kids too. George would do everything, the pick-ups, the parents evenings, the sports days. And they all called him Dad, so his loss was equally as traumatic for all of them. But for Heidi, it hit her particularly hard.

Even now she has grief counselling every week. I think she's just struggling to process her emotions.

She's so, so insecure as well, which I've touched on already, but that is a constant worry to me; how she only seems to see herself and her value based on what's on social media.

To be honest I was quite shocked when she announced she wanted to do The Voice Kids, an ITV singing show that was shown on Saturday night, prime time.

Heidi's a lot like Molly, they both have beautiful voices and Heidi's forever singing around the house, so it made sense to give the show a try. It was something Heidi actually really pushed for, even though she does have such huge insecurities. We initially went to audition for the show in 2018, but she became very overwhelmed and she didn't make it through. It was a really stressful process, and just seeing how upset she was, knowing her confidence was low, was really emotional for me. I felt guilty that she was even in that situation – despite the fact she so desperately wanted to do it at the time.

As far as I was concerned she could've left it there and I would've been just as proud of her, but a couple of years later she insisted she wanted to give it another go. I wasn't sure at all, but her singing teacher said she had grown up a lot so I reluctantly agreed. And she smashed the audition and got through to the televised show.

The thing is with Heidi, if she's with her mates, or she's with us in the living room, she's a real show-off. But put her on stage and that all seems to disappear. Anyway, when it came to filming, she got so upset during the rehearsals, she could barely speak. Her anxiety got the better of her.

"Let's go home, baby girl" I begged her, fearing the whole process was supposed to be fun and it was turning into quite the opposite. "Nothing's worth you feeling like this."

"I don't want to go, Mum", she wept. "I don't want to disappoint myself."

It broke my heart hearing her speak like that. She was still so young, and regardless of what an amazing opportunity it was, I couldn't bear to see her so sad.

I was happy to go home but I knew she was desperate to at least try so I changed tack.

"I'm more than OK with leaving now, Heidi", I said gently. "But I'm scared you'll regret it if you don't at least give it a try. If you hit a bum note, what's the worst that will happen? No one's gonna die, the ceiling won't fall in, people will just look at you and think you're the strongest little girl in the world."

It seemed to spur her on. She stepped foot on that stage and blew everyone away. We then just had to make sure she'd be able to go through with it when the cameras were rolling for real.

Of course it didn't quite go to plan.

When it came to filming the actual show Heidi started crying and couldn't stop. The poor child was so scared and overwhelmed with nerves.

It took an amazing producer called Claire to calm her down, but she was so upset that I just wanted to get her out of there. Heidi told me later she was struggling to breathe in the panic of it all.

I felt like such a bad mum in that moment. Although ITV and the producers were amazing and in no way were they forcing her to do anything, as a mother I was really freaking out. Eventually I was asked to leave the room so Claire could have a bit of time with Heidi.

Whatever she said in those moments worked wonders because next thing I know I was standing next to Emma Willis in a room backstage, while Heidi stepped out in front of the huge live audience to a collective, compassionate "Awwww!"

Now I know Heidi's cute and all, but I was a bit intrigued why the audience were reacting like that, until I saw her little face on the monitor. Her nose was bright red, her eyes were swollen, she had a tissue in her hand – they were reacting to how upset she was! But my God she pulled it out of the bag. She was amazing and once she got over her stage fright she was brilliant, even if she didn't quite make it through to the final.

Even now she says she'd like a career as a singer, but I want to keep an eye on her because I do worry about her anxiety. She's said herself she's terrified of most things, and that's true.

In an interview once she claimed, "I'm scared of everything. Heights, spiders, clowns – how can anyone not be scared of clowns?! I'm height-a-phobic, spider-phobic, clown-a-phobic, I'm everything-a-phobic!" At least she has a sense of humour about it!

But I know she's suffered a lot, mostly as a result of her father being absent, so I understand why she's so fragile. She's definitely got daddy issues, but she's the kindest, sweetest most talented girl and I know she'll succeed in whatever she wants to do.

Incidentally, I did ask her what she wanted to be when she grows up and she said… "I wanna be Molly-Mae."

Yep, my 15-year-old wants to be an influencer just like the Love Island star.

Shock.

*****

And now to my baby boy, Max. My funny, sweet, sensitive lad, who has struggled so much with his ADHD in recent years, but since moving back up north he seems to have found some peace. During the pandemic we really struggled with him. I remember he smashed up his bedroom once in such a rage, he was so frustrated with the lockdowns. He's also lashed out at me and Ryan a few times but I accept it's part of his condition and it's all about us helping him to manage it.

When we moved we actually struggled to find him a school place for quite a while, so he was home tutored. But we knew we had to make sure he was socialising with boys his age, so we sent him to a boxing club. Well, would you believe it – he thrived! It's something he absolutely loves and it's given him a whole new friendship circle as well as a lot more confidence.

And confidence is key with Max. Growing up as the only boy in a gang of four girls, I've often worried if he feels left out, or outnumbered. And I used to hope that George would be the one to teach him, show him the ways after Mark left. Of course, in hindsight I wouldn't want Max to be anything like George, but at the time, especially before the violence got really bad, I would be so proud when I'd see him and George together.

But at the same time, George could be terribly cruel to the children. It broke my heart when he did it. He'd try and belittle them, embarrass them and make them feel small. And yet, if someone was to pick on them, George would take a bullet for them. And that's what made it so hard to walk away. When he was good, he was *brilliant*. We all lived to make him happy, we craved those moments when he was on form. We lived for his approval.

I still feel so much guilt that the kids, and Max, in particular being a boy, had to experience all that. And I know he felt bereft when George died too, as to him it was like another man leaving, much like Heidi.

I'm so grateful now that he and Ryan have such a good relationship and that Ryan knows how to handle him.

But it must be hard for the kids growing up in a household where people know who your mum is. I remember being really upset by a very unsavoury incident that happened when Max was 11. I actually wrote about it in my new! magazine column, where I share stories from my life on a weekly basis with readers.

I wrote: "I was shaken to the core last week by a very unpleasant incident that occurred between my Max and a young lad he knows while the pair were playing on the Xbox. They were communicating over their headsets and when Max beat the boy at the game, this lad took the defeat badly and yelled at Max, 'I'm going to rape your druggie mum.' Max was upset and confused as he's just 11 and he doesn't know what the word rape means."

I continued, "I've asked to speak to the boy's parents about it, as I will not have my children bullied because of who I am and what my past was. It was a terrifying wake-up call, it proves it's not just online trolls who can attack – the verbal word is so powerful and damaging I feel like no one's safe, not even my 11-year-old baby who just wanted to play his computer game."

Even now I can't believe that actually happened and I hate the fact that my kids have to hear the word 'druggie' in association with me. I've always, always been honest with them about my past and so they know the drill, but when other people bring it up – especially fellow children who I can only assume heard it from their parents – it's really upsetting.

I know as Max gets older he understands it more. I know he doesn't harbour any resentment about our past and I think the stability of having Ryan around makes the world of difference to him. He's a boy who needs a father, put it like that. And while I can be both parents as much as possible, there's no real substitute for that man-on-man time that I know he cherishes with Ryan. They're a little duo now, and I love to see it. Better late than never.

*****

# My World

Little DJ is another one I watch out for, only because, as I've said already, I worry she's struggled in light of her dad's death. I still cry thinking about the fact she'll never see him again and – unlike the other kids – she doesn't even have the option to.

I worry about how it will affect her going forward to know the details of his demise, the grubbiness of it all. I worry that she'll read this when she's older having had no real idea of what he was capable of and hate me for putting it down on paper. But I do try to be open with her about the reasons she didn't see her daddy in the last year of his life. And, in trying to introduce George's father to her now, I feel some sense of satisfaction that I'm doing the right thing when it comes to keeping her in tune with her heritage and her race.

She does still act out and she's incredibly clingy to me – she will still sleep in the same bed as Ryan and I just because she doesn't like being on her own. Soon after George died she would complain that her bedroom was haunted and she didn't like to be alone.

She'll have temper tantrums and screaming fits like most young children do from time to time, but I sense hers are rooted in the frustration about her dad. And even though Ryan has basically raised her since she was little and she absolutely adores him, I know losing her real father will have a profound effect on her growing up.

I just have to keep talking to her, acknowledging what she's feeling and never dismiss her trauma just because she's young. She's got a smart, beautiful little head on those shoulders and I know she'll grow up to be a well adjusted human – but that's on me as well, I need to keep working with her to make sure that happens after everything she's been through.

It's so hard to deal with five different children: that's five different personalities, five different needs, five different wants. It's difficult to juggle. But I don't know any better as I've always had kids. I've been a single mother for a far longer period of time than I've been with a man! And I wouldn't change it for the world.

Call me whatever you want, shame me for my past, mock me for my choices, I don't care. But if you come for my kids, then we'll have a problem. Luckily they've grown up to ignore the background noise. They know our truth and they know exactly what we've survived as a family. To say I'm proud of them is an understatement. They are a credit to me and their dads, and to Ryan who's stepped up to father five children, none of which are his own, in the most incredible, kind, patient way.

I'm a very lucky woman to have the family I do. No matter what we've been through and no matter how hard times get, we're always there for each other – and when all else goes to shit, that's the only thing that matters.

## 23

# Keep The Faith

It was only a few weeks after George passed away that I threw myself wholeheartedly into Hillsong.

For those who don't know, Hillsong is an evangelical Christian church, with hundreds of venues across the world and it really became famous when Justin Bieber, Kanye and the Kardashian family joined. Personally, I love it. It gave me an enormous sense of peace in those dark days and even now I'm not sure I believe the claims from some of the former members calling it a 'cult'.

There were reports of historic abuse and controlling behaviour, a bit like in Scientology, the controversial Hollywood religion headed up by Tom Cruise, but I've never, ever seen anything like that – all I can confirm is it got me through a really hard time.

I took the kids down to a service one sunny day in the August of 2019, it was only a month or so after George died and I knew deep down I was looking for something, anything, to help ease the pain.

At first, I didn't think the kids were keen. It took a bit of persuading, but when we got there it was clear just how uplifting and empowering it was going to be. I was immediately hooked.

There are just six Hillsong churches in the UK, and one was in Tonbridge, where we were still living at the time. My neighbours had been urging me to go for a while, so on that particular Sunday I just bit the bullet and went for it. It felt like fate having a service so close to us, it was like it was meant to be.

It was fantastic. As soon as I walked in I felt like I was in a rock concert or something. The singing was joyous, the preachers were so inspirational and the whole vibe was completely down to earth. No offence to Catholic services, but having been to a couple of them myself, I know they can send you to sleep. They're not that modern, they're still quite stuffy and that's everything Hillsong wasn't.

Walking in that room, I felt like the pastor was talking directly to me. Of all the people in there, I'm sure everyone felt the same, but I really felt a connection to his words and I was crying my eyes out listening to him speak. The annoying thing is I don't recall now the exact words he said, but isn't that often the way? You don't always remember what was said – but you remember how it made you feel.

Well, I felt so moved. And the music lifted me unlike anything I'd experienced before. I know I was fragile because of what had happened with George, but I feel like no matter what state of mind I was in – positive or negative – it was only ever going to make me feel even better just by being there. I really needed something in that moment. And I know the kids did too, even if they were still a bit young to appreciate it fully. We started going fairly regularly and I can honestly say it was a saviour to me.

# Keep The Faith

Knowing how George had died, the suddenness of it, the brutal way in which he just left the earth, I'd become so, so scared of death. And Hillsong gave me an enormous amount of comfort, as does my faith in general, to think there might be something else beyond this life. I'm terrified of not being with my kids and not watching them grow up, it scares the hell out of me, so I cling to every bit of hope I can when it comes to mortality and the afterlife. I can't fathom a world where you just perish into dust and no longer exist.

Of course the press got wind of my trips to Hillsong and the headlines inevitably started screaming things like: 'Kerry's Found God in the Wake of Hubby's Death!' But the truth is, I've always been incredibly spiritual, I've always believed in a higher power and Jesus Christ and I do identify as a Christian.

I haven't been to Hillsong since I moved up north, simply because I can't find a church nearby. It didn't help that Covid derailed everything and the services went online. I tried it but it didn't work for me. It wasn't the same. For me, that feeling of walking into that service, realising something incredible was happening, and then skipping out of there after, it was like an awakening! I loved the feeling of interaction and togetherness and you do tend to lose that online.

But just because I haven't been to a service, I still say my prayers every day, which people may be surprised to know about me. I'm a big believer in God, whoever that may be. And I love anything historical and biblical, so things like the nativity story, Easter, all those sorts of holidays I celebrate from a religious point of view.

But equally when it comes to religion, I take bits from different places. I love the peace of Buddhism, for instance.

And the forgiveness and story behind Christianity. So I try to take the best parts of different religions and apply them to my everyday life.

I like what suits me and what works for me, you see. It's like when you go to a shop and buy a bikini. I never get the same top and bottom, I always have to mix and match (I'm much bigger up top) – and it's the same with religion, you gotta try on a few things, combine a few elements until the whole outfit comes together.

It's not just religion, though. I'm a firm believer in affirmation, manifestation and gratitudes, which I practice every single day.

I was given the book The Secret years ago and it really spoke to me. I was hanging out with Peter Andre a lot at the time and in those days that was like his bible. He seemed to live by it.

I wasn't as invested at that point, I never followed it but as I watched all these great things happen to Pete and seeing how it seemed to be working for him, it did pique my interest.

The concept is pretty simple, it's all about the law of attraction, that you can think something into happening. The idea is that you visualise everything you want in life, and the energy those manifestations put into the world will ensure what you want comes true. It's not some sort of mumbo jumbo hippy idea, this is a book that's been read by over 300m people worldwide, and so many readers have found success with it.

Despite getting rave reviews from Pete, it was actually George who really got me into it in a big way. He was massively into stuff like that and was a big believer in manifestation. We'd watch videos from people like Bob Proctor and David Icke and Lisa Nichols, all best-selling self-help authors who contributed to the documentary film version of The Secret too.

# Keep The Faith

We could sit there watching for hours on end, fascinated by what these people had to say, as we kept imagining a better life for ourselves and how we could go about finding it.

For instance, we'd tape a cheque up on the mirror, made payable to us for £10m, and look at it every single day, manifesting that one day we'd be able to cash it in for real.

George would listen to various different podcasts about the subject as he'd be doing the housework (he loved to clean), but the problem with George was he expected these things to land in his lap.

Yes, it's all very well sticking the cheque on the mirror, but you have to be a grafter too. You have to believe these things will happen for you – and then you have to take the steps to actually *make* it happen.

I really feel like I do that. If I want something, I'll put it into the universe – and then I'll go out and make it a reality.

I once did a vision board, in which I wrote down all the things I wanted to achieve. On that board I put a big house, (tick), a Lamborghini, (tick), my own clothing range, which eventually became Kerry's Boutique, (so, tick), I also wrote down that I was a non-smoker – which I now officially am. It all happened! So there's definitely something in it.

But then I should know, I've been manifesting things since I was a kid.

I remember a vision I had at an airport once. I was looking at a TV screen and I saw Brian performing with Westlife, and I thought, 'He's gonna be my ex-husband one day'.

It's weird how you tend to create your own reality sometimes.

*****

And it's not just The Secret and vision boards I swear by. I follow a lot of similar programmes and I really feel like my studying and knowledge of them has given me back my self-worth.

When I went to rehab once all those years ago, I got my book from the AA that I still refer to now. It's absolutely covered in post-it notes and highlighted chapters and if I'm ever at a low ebb, or I feel like I need a bit of guidance, I'll refer back to it.

I also write in a gratitude book every day.

There's a book called Think and Grow Rich, by Napoleon Hill. Bob Proctor recommended people read it, study it, learn from it, and that's exactly what I did. To me, it was a bit like my university education, that. At the end of studying it you have to write an essay about what you've learnt. It's all about getting back what you put into the world. That book is my bible. It absolutely changed my life. Financially, emotionally, mentally – it changed everything. I'd highly recommend it to anyone who feels like they're in a hopeless situation. It really gave me some self-belief. I've always known I can get back to the top from the very bottom, and I'm living proof it worked.

When I split up with George, I realised I was more than enough for my kids and it took me a long time to get there, but it was mainly because of my self-help books, my manifestations and my belief in a higher power.

But like I said, it's not just about wishing and hoping and believing, it's about hard work as well. And you do have to be selfish to an extent. I've put so much hard work into myself, especially into forgiving myself for my mistakes.

In fact that's where the bible has helped me in particular. In helping me to forgive myself for the person I was. Staying out all night, partying, drinking, snorting. You read these stories about me from back in the day and they do make me sound so erratic, and of course I was for a time. I was on a bad path. But I forgive myself now. I have to.

*****

Faith plays a huge part in my day to day life. Huge. If you haven't got faith, then really, what have you got? Faith is hope. Yes, I've got my past, I've got my misery and faith is what's got me through. Faith in myself and faith that there's something bigger out there.

I know I've been put here by a greater power for a reason. Sometimes I wonder who can go through what I've been through and survive the way I have. There's a reason I now sit in a £3m house, having been broke and shattered just two years earlier.

I know I have angels, put it that way.

I remember one incident, in the dark days of being married to Mark Croft, when I passed out after a coke binge. When I came to, I saw I had a group of angels around me.

I was lying there, coughing and frothing and fitting, but I sensed them immediately. And despite the indescribable pain and guilt I was in, having just put my life in danger, I've never felt love like it.

It was this warm glow that I can't explain. I was absolutely surrounded by love. These floating figures in white were stood around me, bringing me back to life. It was lovely. Even now it gives me goosebumps thinking about it. And it reminds me that there is something out there.

I know religion is polarising, it's literally started wars but to me it's a huge part of who I am. I wouldn't say I'm "praise Jesus!" religious in a preachy way, I'd never tell anyone who they should worship or what they should believe in, but I personally do believe in a higher power. I think Jesus Christ is cool, he's great, but I don't have to tell people about it all the time.

To be fair, if I could have a dinner party with anyone, dead or alive, Jesus himself would be at my table. I'd ask him if Mary really was a virgin! (I'm only joking, that's a terrible thing to say!)

But… just so you know, JC, if you *do* tell me, I won't ruin thousands of years of history by revealing the secret in this book.

But do spill when we have that dinner party, yeah?

## 24
# Whole Again

If life has taught me anything, it's that I'm a survivor. Having sat here and written this book, reliving some of the most horrific things that could ever happen to a woman, I'm amazed I'm still alive. I look back and wonder how I got through any of it and how the hell I can still be here to tell the tale.

And what a tale, eh? I truly believe my life story should be made into a film. Seriously, not even Steven Spielberg could come up with a screenplay this mental, but yet it all happened to me. Sadly, there was no one there to yell 'cut' and stop the cameras rolling when the scenes got tough. In real life there is no safety net, no break in the action – all you can do is experience the trauma and get through it.

And boy oh boy, have I been through it.

But everything I've been through has helped me become the strong, happy, healthy person I've become. And in particular, the following people have been especially instrumental in shaping the woman I am today.

273

# Kerry Katona

## My three husbands

To Brian McFadden: My learning curve. I was young, in love and living a fairytale. Only it was just that: a fairytale. Magical, but never destined to be my happily ever after. However, I became a mother thanks to Brian. And for me, holding Molly in my arms on the day she was born was the true beginning of my journey. Nothing mattered before she came along. So in that respect, regardless of the heartbreak I endured when that marriage ended, I'll be forever grateful that I met Brian, married him and had two of his children.

To Mark Croft: My big mistake. A marriage that spelt only trouble from the start. A bad choice that resulted in two beautiful kids – the only thing I don't regret about that particular union. I had to reach my lowest point with that man in order to wake up, get sober and pull myself together. A lot of my choices around that time could have left me dead. And believe me, he was not a fella worth dying for. But marrying him reminded me to trust my instincts and remember my worth.

And to George Kay: My survival story. Surviving not just the physical and emotional abuse he subjected me to, but surviving the heartache of loving – and losing – a man so troubled. Surviving the pressure of keeping up appearances, hiding secrets so big they weigh you down to the point where you can barely stand. Surviving the trauma of watching my kids go through hell and knowing it was my fault for allowing that to happen. I suppose in many ways the only thing I didn't survive is the guilt of what I put them through. I'll never get over that.

# Whole Again

I will carry it with me for the rest of my life. But remembering that each day ensures I'll never, ever allow something like that to happen again.

## Ryan

Never before has a man changed my life in the way Ryan has. Completely and utterly for the better. I have enough ambition and drive to make it on my own, but with Ryan by my side, I can take on the world and then some. He's the first man I've truly wanted, as opposed to needed, and that's incredibly important. The Kerry before Ryan would rely on men, rather than herself. Now, I know I can make it on my own if need be. But the fact I *choose* to go through life with Ryan simply speaks volumes about the positive influence he's had on me and the enormous love I have for him.

He found me when I was feeling strong – like attracts like, clearly – and he supported me when I became weak again. He lifted me up after George's death in a way I'll never ever forget. I know I'll be with Ryan forever and for the first time in my life, I have absolutely no doubt about that at all.

## My kids

No matter how bleak life can get, I truly believe everyone has something to live for. I'm lucky enough to have five things. Molly, Lilly, Heidi, Max and DJ are and always will be my entire world. No one else comes close to those kids. Becoming a mother was my dream and to fulfill that dream five times over, birthing the most perfect little humans, well, I still pinch myself.

They're the ones I get up every day for. They're the ones I graft my arse off to provide for. The ones who can do my head in but yet I'd take a bullet for, no questions asked. I really believe I've survived everything I've been through because they need me to be here for them. I would have died, almost certainly by my own hand, if it wasn't for the children and the fact they need their mum. There's no way I'm giving up and leaving them in this world without a mother and my only goal in life now is to be the best parent I can possibly be.

In the words of my old mate Bryan Adams, everything I do, I do it for you, kids.

## Me.

Of all the relationships I've had, be it with men, my mum, my kids, or my colleagues – the most important of all is the one I have with myself. I've marched to my own beat since I was a kid, and I continue to do so to this day. I'm outspoken, I'm honest and I'll scream my truth from the rooftops so my voice is heard loud and clear. I'm nothing if not authentic.

But it's taken a lot of work for me to really love *me*. Throughout my life I felt I deserved the pain and chaos I inevitably received. I thought violence and abuse was normal, so I never seemed to question if I deserved better. But I *did* deserve better. We all do. I've spent many, many nights working on myself and learning to love Kerry Katona. Bipolar, bankruptcy, addiction, flaws and all. But now I can stand here, a gorgeous man on my arm, two Lamborghinis in my driveway, a career I'm super proud of and money in the bank and finally say: "I made it. And I'm bloody brilliant to boot."

# Whole Again

Having the kids and Ryan by my side has made it a lot easier to love myself, sure. In fact finally seeing what they see in me has been an incredibly beautiful breakthrough. But the bottom line is, no one can save you but yourself.

It took every ounce of inner strength I had to walk away from George, but I did it. It was never easy. In fact surviving the hell he put me through has been the hardest thing I've ever, ever gone through, but here I am, still standing. Finally free.

To any women or men out there who can identify with my story, please know: you're not alone. When you're at rock bottom, don't give up. There's always, always a way out. A better life can be found if you have the right help and support to hand. Sometimes that support comes in the form of a charity, sometimes in friends and family, and sometimes from a complete stranger. But it's there. You are never, *ever* alone.

Trust me, I've been there.

I've survived.

Now watch me thrive.

# USEFUL CONTACTS

**Women's Aid**
A grassroots federation working together to provide
life-saving services in England and build a future
where domestic abuse is not tolerated.

www.womensaid.org.uk

**Tommy's**
Dedicated to finding causes and treatments to save
babies' lives as well as providing trusted pregnancy
and baby loss information and support.

www.tommys.org

**FRANK**
For facts, support and advice on drugs
and alcohol.

www.talktofrank.com

**Mind**
Offering information and advice to people
with mental health issues.

www.mind.org.uk

*Other organisations are available.*